The Tomorrow Project Anthology

Conversations About the Future

Cory Doctorow
will.i.am
Douglas Rushkoff
Brian David Johnson

Sponsors of Tomorrow.™

ISBN 13 978-1-934053-45-4

Publisher: Richard Bowles
Program Manager: Joe Zawadsky
Editorial input and copyediting: John R. Douglas
Composition: MPS Limited, a Macmillan Company
Cover Design + Artwork: Shannon E Thomas for **frog**

Library of Congress Cataloging in Publication Data:

Printed in United States of America

10 9 8 7 6 5 4 3 2

Second printing, November 2011

Contents

Introduction

Chapter 1

Introduction: How to Change the Future

—by Brian David Johnson

Let's get one thing straight: the future is not set. The future is not some fixed point just over the horizon that we are all helplessly hurtling towards. No. We are not powerless. The future is not written. The future is made every day by the actions of people. Because of this I have always believed that everyone should be an active participant in the future. If we are all making it and we are all going to live in it then why not do something about it individually.

Now you might argue that you alone cannot have any real or meaningful effect on the future. You are just one person. What could you do to help shape the future? Well, I'll tell you—you can do a lot.

Earlier this year I was in London, England talking with Cory Doctorow. Cory has a novella in this collection. I've been a big fan of his writing and work for many years. Cory is not just a bestselling science fiction author he's also a passionate advocate for the rights of people. Basically he is a welcome voice of sanity and humanism in an increasingly complex world. So, I was sitting in Cory's book-lined office in the Hackney neighborhod of London and I asked him a question:

How can we change the future?

I had been on a campaign for all of 2011 asking people this same question. I had traveled around the world and asked economists, synthetic biologists, science fiction authors, futurists, professors, government officials and corporate executives. On that day in London I still had no answer. What I did have was a lot of people who were mad at me. Turns out that little question made a lot of people really angry. What I had thought was a pretty practical question turned into a lightning rod for passion and purpose around shaping the future. Don't get me wrong, I had some really good conversations but no one had given me an answer that satisfied me.

When I asked Cory the question he had the same initial reaction as the rest. He wasn't sure you could really ask a question like that nor could a person honestly answer it. I settled back in my chair and got ready for a good long argument when Cory stopped and said:

> *I guess the way you change the future is to change people's narrative. Change the story people have imagined the future will be. Change that and you change the future. Everything else is far too complicated and out of a single person's control—but just change the story we tell ourselves about the future and you change the future itself.*

Now that's an answer!

For the last decade I've been writing science fiction based on science fact as a way to explore our possible futures. More recently over the last five years I've been teaching this process. I've also been lucky enough to work with a collection of passionate and dedicated educators and story tellers who are using this process to actually build better products and technology.

My goal throughout these years has been to somehow make a better future. I believe if we can envision the future we want then we can work to build it. At the same time, if we can envision the future we want to avoid, we can actively try to prevent it. And this is where you come in (you had to know this was coming . . .)

As anyone will tell you, a good story is about people. A science fiction story based upon real science is still about people. It's not about the science or technology. It's about the effect that the science has on people and the world around them.

When two people read the same story then they can have a conversation about that science and the effect of that science on the world around us. They can talk about it. They can talk about what they liked and what they didn't like. One might say, "Well, I'd like a world where this might happen or I think it would be better if it went like this . . ." Perhaps the other person then argues that they'd like an altogether different future.

The conversation goes on from there. We've all had them. It could be about a story or a movie or a comic we've read. But we've all done it. In that conversation we can change the narrative. We can change the story that we tell ourselves about the future. If we do that and we do that with enough people we can actually change the future for the better.

That's what the Tomorrow Project is all about—conversations about the future. And through these conversations we can change the future.

Over the past year I've had some really interesting conversations with some fascinating people for the Tomorrow Project. You can find the videos and podcasts here: http://techresearch.intel.com/tomorrowproject.aspx. I spend so much time talking to people about the future that I've been asked who my favorite conversationalist is. The answer sometimes surprises people. I'm a big fan of Carl Sagan, Richard Feynman and other great popularizeres of science. But my favorite conversationalist is Dick Cavett. He was just plain good at having a conversation with people.

If you don't know Cavett, he was a talk show host starting in the 1960s. During that time he had almost everyone on his show. He talked to people like Groucho Marx, Jimi Hendrix, Salvador Dali, Woody Allen, and Orson Welles. When you watch the July 1970 conversation between Cavett and Welles you are really watching two men have a conversation, neither knowing exactly where it is going but both of them having a heck of a good time.

What I love about Cavett is that he really did talk to people. He didn't interview them. There were no set questions, no question and answer. In his autobiography *Talk Show* he defined what he thought a conversation was this way:

> *"Conversation is when people simply talk; not take a test on the air with Q and A. It's when something said spontaneously prompts a thought and a reply in someone else. When several people's talk moves around a subject, changes directions and produces spontaneous and entertaining comments and unexpected insights, and takes surprising turns." (Times Books, 2010)*

The Tomorrow Project Anthology is full of these kinds of conversations. When we started talking to people about the future based upon science that was being developed today we had no idea where the conversations would lead. When you ask someone like Cory Doctorow about the future of computing and security you really can't know what's going to happen. His story *The Knights of the Rainbow Table* not only provides a fascinating picture of a possible future but it also reveals unexpected insights and surprising turns. What surprised me the most was how human the story became. In the beginning it was a grand story about what could happen but in the end it became about the personal effect that a world without passwords could have on a person's wellbeing.

Similarly, for the section of the book called *The Tomorrow Project-Seattle* we put out an open call for stories based on real research going on inside Intel and the University of Washington and we had no idea what would come back. I do see the collection of these stories as a conversation amongst many people producing spontaneous and entertaining comments. Each one is like a request for the future.

Finally we included two essays and conversations I've had this year with will.i.am and Douglas Rushkoff. Both of them are engaging futurists and both are equally as passionate about the future of education and how we might change the narrative of how we think about education relating to the rapid growth of technology.

Like Cavett said, a conversation is *when several people's talk moves around a subject, changes directions and produces spontaneous and entertaining comments and unexpected insights, and takes surprising turns.* The Tomorrow Project is just that, a collection of people talking around a subject: the future. Their conversations change direction and produce spontaneous and entertaining comments. They also give us unexpected insights and surprising turns. The goal of the Tomorrow Project is to have conversations about the future so that we can make that future better. I'd like to invite you to join the conversation and change the future.

—Brian David Johnson
Los Angeles, California

Knights of the Rainbow Table

Chapter 2

Knights of the Rainbow Table

—Cory Doctorow (doctorow@craphound.com)

The day that our lawyer told us that the DA had added a federal conspiracy charge to the rap sheet, I immediately flashed on what Abbie Hoffman said when they served papers on him for the Chicago 8 conspiracy trial: "Conspiracy? Man, we can't even agree on where to have dinner!" I would have said it, but just after Moszkowski gave us the bad news, our waitress showed up and asked Sir Tristan what he wanted to order.

We Knights of the Rainbow Table had always had a problem with restaurants: that problem's name was Sir Tristan Erkko, who was intolerant of lactose, processed carbohydrates, salt, vegans, forks with bent tines and people with poor grammar. Tristan never spoke above a whisper, and he affected a huge mustache that made it impossible for waitresses to read his lips, which made the lengthy negotiations even longer. Normally, the Knights of the Rainbow Table tried to find quiet restaurants where Sir Tristan could dicker at length without having to whisper directly into the server's ear, but Moszkowski had chosen the place, a busy pizza parlor on Telegraph Hill filled with noisy Berkeley kids. I suppose he thought it would allow us to converse without being overheard. He was a paranoid old civil rights fixer, but Knights of the Rainbow Table could have taught him volumes about the practical limits of privacy.

The three of us stared uncomfortably at one another until Tristan had conveyed his exacting pizza parameters, Lady Tracey and Moszkowski took their turns, and then it was my turn.

Here's the truth: I might make fun of Sir Tristan's ordering peccadilloes, I might sneer at Moszkowski's privacy naiveté, I might turn up my nose at the pineapple and anchovies that Lady Tracey eats with such gusto, but the fact is, at least they can all *eat*, which is more than you can say for me.

"I'll have a glass of water," I said, and endured three pairs of eyes looking at me with that mixture of pity and disgust I've come to know so well. My stomach growled at me, a sound I felt to my eyebrows, and I touched my midriff with one bony finger, a feeling like a dried out drum-head, the skin stretched so tight and desiccated that it rustled.

The waitress reached out with a chewed fingernail and tapped the scratched sign on the table that said, "$10 minimum order per customer." I'd already noticed the sign. I slid out the $10 bill I'd placed under my fork and knife and passed it to her. "It's cool," I said.

She rolled her eyes with youthful eloquence and walked off, leaving our conspiracy to get back to business.

"You know," I said, "for a gang of supercriminals, we're a pretty sorry bunch."

Moszkowski said, "I'm going to pretend you didn't say that."

Sir Tristan reached across the table and took my fork and held it up to the light, inspecting the tines and comparing it to his fork. Wordlessly, Lady Tracey handed him her fork, too, and after some deliberation, he picked one and passed the other two back.

Lady Tracey waited until he'd carefully squared the fork up on his napkin, keeping it evenly spaced with his knife and framed by a uniform border of white paper napkin. Then she darted out one hand, snatched the fork he'd so carefully chosen, and licked all its tines, front and back, and returned it to its spot.

Sir Tristan glared at her and then set the fork aside and picked up the remaining three and chose the one with the second-most-uniform tines and once again set to squaring it up on his napkin. I saw the demonic glee light up Lady Tracey's eyes as she made ready to lick this one, too, and I put out my hand and caught her wrist. "Don't," I said. "Come on." My cracked skin rasped over Lady Tracey's smooth fingers and she shuddered involuntarily.

"All right, children," Moszkowski said. "Enough. You're being arraigned tomorrow and I need you all to be on your best behavior. The Computer Fraud and Abuse charges are bad, add the conspiracy count and there's a serious chance you're going to end up in a cell until your trial. None of us want that, do we?"

Here, at last, was something that all the storied Knights of the Rainbow Table could agree upon.

Once upon a time, in the Duchy of Berkeley in the mythical kingdom of Bayarea, three brave knights did swear an oath to fight the forces of trolls, creeps, identity thieves, snoops, spooks and the whole motley army of Internet Evildoers, lo until they breathed their last breath.

We didn't set out to become knights. We set out to test a cluster. A big, big cluster. Tristan got the idea after going to an art installation in which 1,000 antique PCs were networked across row on row of fake Metro wire shelving, each with a 3.5" floppy in its drive. The artist had done some clever mojo to span a single, redundant 1GB filesystem across the whole cluster, which was used to store and retrieve a constantly updating loop of video shot with a single camera fixed into the ceiling, looking down on the exhibition. The artist had hired about a dozen kids on roller-skates to ride around the racks, swapping out floppies as they went corrupt, the video on the big screen juddering every time this happened and the filesystem recovered.

"So my idea was why not build something you know useful out of all the old computer junk around here like a cluster or something?" Tristan always had the least punctuation of anyone I knew, but he made up for this by inserting extra excited spittle between his words as he talked.

"Where would we keep it?" I said. At the time, Tristan and I were sharing a one-bedroom apartment near campus. I slept in the living room. When we had houseguests (itinerant hackers, mostly), they slept on an air mattress on the kitchen floor.

"What about the electric bill?" Tracey said. She'd bossed a colo in Texas before she moved to Berkeley for college. She could quote the formula for calculating the net amperage-per-flop for the chillers from memory. "What about administration? What about backhaul?"

Tristan shrugged and twirled up some of his mustache and stuck it in his mouth. Neither of us took any notice; he'd been doing that since freshman year, when we three had aced a joint project together that led to frequent hanging out and then roommatehood and even a short-lived and mercifully painless romance between Tracey and me. "I don't know but what about a cluster? I mean a big one like a teraflop or bigger I just thought it'd be cool."

We admitted this was so and went on to the next thing and the next and several days went by before Tracey forwarded us both an email about the engineering faculty inheriting a semi-derelict brick factory near the docklands as a bequest on the condition that they not sell it for 10 years. Tristan wrote most of the proposal (he was much better in print than he was in person), Tracey filled in the technical details, and I made the pitch to a prof we all liked and he passed it up the food chain and we ended up with 10,000 square feet— about one tenth of the available square footage.

We rigged the water-cooling ourselves, using sea-water. Our faculty supervisor carefully ensured that he didn't know what we were doing. At first, there were a few other groups that applied for space in the Brick Shithouse (as the factory was instantly dubbed, thanks in part to the faint sewage smell that no amount of airing could get rid of). But no one really wanted to haul ass out to the Shithouse and soon we had the place all to ourselves. Our 10,000 square feet quickly grew to nearly the whole building, row on row of PCs of every description salvaged from campus and nearby, wiped and enlinuxed, networked and left to wheeze for as long as they went on working. At any given time, about 15 percent of the cluster was nonfunctional, and we made good use of impressionable freshmen whom we sourced via Craigslist and threw at the problem machines, letting them keep whatever they could fix. This sounds zero-sum: if they took everything they fixed, wouldn't that mean that the dead machines would disappear? But fixing computers is like eating potato chips: most people can't stop at just one. Each one is a perfect puzzle of vendor defects, material wear, capricious software ghouls, and emergent phenomena. The brain-reward for restoring a genuinely threadbare PC to active duty was more psychotropic than anything for sale in People's Park.

How much power did we have? Less than Google; more than all the radio astronomers in Europe, combined. The number isn't important: to buy an hour's worth of as much CPU as we assembled in today's cloud marketplace, you'd have to work for two hours at minimum wage. Our pizza waitress could blow us out of the water and still have enough left for rent, assuming she had a roommate.

What did we do with all that power? At first, we just entered various big computation projects, throwing our farm at Folding@Home to do some handily parallelizable fast Fourier transforms in order to help fight AIDS and cancer and such. This is extremely altruistic work, but it's not very interesting from a research perspective. As interesting as it was to step into the frigid Shithouse and be engulfed in the white-noise jetwash of all the computers, we weren't learning anything about our cluster or its individual components.

It was Tracey who decided to go after rainbow tables, these being something of a holy grail in the security field. It was Tracey who made us the Knights of the Rainbow Table, and set our destiny in motion. But I forgive her.

To understand rainbow tables, you need to understand hash-functions. These are fundamental units of the cryptographic arts, and what they do is easy to grasp but requires either a large amount of math or a large amount of faith. For the purposes of this account, I will go with faith.

Take it on faith, if you will that there is a way to convert one blob of text (the password) into another blob of text (the hash) such that it is mathematically certain that:

(a)   No amount of work will permit you to determine which password is responsible for creating which hash; and

(b)   The same password always produces the same hash.

If you will permit me this axiom, we can proceed without equations. Should you require equations to accept it, by all means, go look them up and then come back, you faithless wretch.

Hashing functions are bipolar: you can never determine what password created them, but you can always redetermine the hash by feeding the same password back to it–they are mysterious and deterministic all at once.

Imagine that you have created a "good" password: that is, one that does not appear in any dictionary that has been written, nor any dictionary that some clever person might create (say, by taking all the words in the English language and substituting 1 for L and 3 for E and so forth). You visit a website and the server says, "Please give me a good password." You supply it. The server computes its hash and sticks that in a database, and throws away your original password.

The next time you visit the site, it will ask you for your password again. When you provide it, it runs it through the hashing function again (again discarding your original password, which it does not want to know!), and compares the hashed value with the stored hash on file. If they match, it knows that you have entered the password correctly–but it still doesn't know what the password is!

A computer that only knows hashes and not passwords is a secure little beast, because even if the file of hashes leaks into the wide world, there's nothing a hacker can do with them. Even if she's captured the hash of your WiFi password or your banking password or your ereader password, it will do her no good: she can feed them to the WiFi network or the bank or the ereader without gain. In order to gain access the hacker needs to know the password, not its hash. Thus a computer can be secured with a minimum of secrecy, and that's good, because secrets are very hard to keep (more on this anon).

Think of hashed passwords as the language of a dead culture with no progeny, a remarkable, forgotten people who had an equivalent word for every word in every contemporary language and even for our non-words and nonsense and who left a key for translating our written phrases into theirs, but with no key by which we might go in the opposite direction. As these foreign words have no cognates with our own, there is no way to guess, merely by reading a word in Hashese, what its contemporary equivalent might be.

Enter the rainbow table. Imagine that you fed a dictionary into the hashing algorithm and made a table of the hashed equivalent of every word, and even non-words, such as words in combination, words with simple substitutions, slang, vernacular, foreign words, common phrases. Then, having captured a password's hash, you could compare it with every one of those hashed words— look it up in your handy English-Hashese/Hashese-English dictionary–and out pops the secret password, no longer a secret. Now you have the password, which is all you need to successfully impersonate its owner to some naive computer, and mischief awaits.

"What would we do with rainbow tables I'm no crook," Tristan muttered from under his mustache, as he idly punched the product ID off a potentially faulty network card into Google to see if anyone had written alternative drivers for it.

Tracey started to answer, but just then one of our undergrad technicians came to the door of the Shithouse's little office, reporting a fault in the cooling system. The cooling system had a *lot* of faults, because water-cooling systems that use sea-water are just stupid, given that sea-water gradually eats everything that contains it, and what it doesn't eat, it chokes with a sclerotic crust of dried salts. Not that we had any choice, because running traditional chillers would have clobbered the Shithouse's annual budget in a matter of weeks, and without aggressive cooling, the place would spike at 60' C in about five minutes, and then it would be a race to see whether the assembled computers fused and died before they could start a fire that killed us all.

Cooling took priority.

When Tracey came back–it was a minor pump problem that we'd all fixed a dozen times and it was mostly just a matter of knowing where to kick and how hard–she said, "Why rainbow tables? Two reasons: first, they are cool, and; second, they parallelize."

That was the kicker, parallelization. A parallelizable problem is one that can be worked on in lots of different places because no step relies on the output from a previous step. Think of stuffing envelopes with friends: one group of friends can address envelopes, another can fill them, and a third can run them through the postage meter. That's pretty parallizable–if you finish with the meter before the stuffing group is done, you can grab a stack of metered envelopes and start stuffing, too. In theory, one slow doofus won't leave a roomful of people sitting around, fuming.

Now, compare that with a serial task, like assembling a jet engine on an assembly line. First, Alice screws on one dingus, then Bill attaches a dingus to that, and Carol attaches a dingus to *that*, and so on, all the way to Zeke, fitting the cowling at the other end of the assembly line. If Alice had a wild night last night and is dragging her ass as a result, Bob, Carol and the rest, yea, unto Zeke are going to be stuck with thumbs firmly planted up their alimentary canals. It might be possible to redesign a jet engine factory to run with more parallel tasks–think of the famed Japanese car companies where small teams assemble whole cars, where one team's dragassing doesn't hold up the factory–but there's a lot of computation where the next step depends on the previous one and the more of that there is, the less you can do with a big parallel cluster.

Of course, there's always some extent to which problems are serial. If there's one guy who's really slow with the address labels, eventually, you're all going to be sitting around waiting for him to finish off his sheet, looking meaningfully at your watches and trying to figure out when the last bus goes.

The Shithouse was full of computers which were, basically, that guy. We didn't discriminate when it came to the rescue animals we took in, nursed to health and set to productive use. The basements and dorm rooms and storage lockers of Berkeley vomited forth a steady stream of junk hardware, stuff that the granoloid masses couldn't bear to send to a landfill. Every time CNN showed another exposé featuring blistered, engoitered Chinese kids laboring over acid vats to strip apart ewaste, we got a fresh shipment of guilt and shame and obsolescence.

Combine that with the screaming doubling curve that computer power rides and you got our shelves, where a given computer might be, quite literally, a million times faster than its neighbor (and like as not, it would be consuming a tenth of the power: talk about eco-guilt, we were a one-building carbon crime wave). We had heterogeneity for days, and with that salmagundi came any number of chewy, interesting clustering problems: Which computers should be in charge of working (translating passwords into hashes), and which computers should be in charge of apportioning work? How do you index what's on which computer, and what do you do about recovering a computer's lost work when it dies? Should more common words be stored on faster computers, or more computers, or both? Or does figuring out which password to put where cost more than we'd save by just dumping passwords into computers at random? These are meaty and interesting subjects and we waged arguments back and forth and up and down about them and wrote feverish code to prove our points of view and never got around to writing up any papers for publication, though we sure started plenty. We could have had an ACM journal dedicated to us: *Journal of Incomplete Research Into Distributed Computing.*

The Rainbow Tables Project had been up and running for a month when Tristan called me from work–he had a wage-slave gig fine-tuning some semi-fraudulent search engine optimization tools at a doomed Oakland startup where he was (get this) the best adjusted programmer on staff.

"I'm thinking of worm trails or ant trails or something like that," he said.

"Nice to hear from you, too, Tristan," I said. We didn't use phones for voice-calls much, various IMs being much cleaner, cryptographically sound, and suited to multitasking. But sometimes Tristan needed to say things aloud to make sure he knew them. But his phone manner was dreadful.

"So when you look up a password you just ask a random computer and if it doesn't have it it asks a random computer and so on and so on until it finds the password. Then the computer with the password tells the next computer and it tells the next and it tells the next and they all store the passwords. Like a pheromone trail. Like ants. So the more you ask for a password the more available it becomes the more pathways there are to it like. It gets more robust the more you use it. Plus we'll be able to see which passwords are commonest over time because the network will evolve to match them." I could hear the spittle flying. He was on a roll.

And he was right. Tracey saw it right away and helped me with a formal proof. But even before I'd finished that, Tristan was coding it, Tracey was debugging it and I was writing test cases for it and you know what? It worked.

Moszkowski sends us email in the clear, no encryption. He relies on the security of his home and office networks and the interconnections between his ISPs and ours to protect and secure our communications. Moszkowski hasn't figured out yet that all that stuff is an open book or if he's figured it out, he hasn't felt it in his guts or his blood or his balls or wherever you need to feel a hard truth before you really know it.

"I'm still looking for a technical expert, someone I can put on the stand who can explain the socially beneficial aspects of your work. None of the names you've suggested have panned out. This is important, guys. It sure would have helped if you'd published or given some learned presentations at big conferences or something. I want to put you in front of the judge as noble security researchers who worked in the service of a better world, but I can only do that if I can find someone other than you to say it."

The conversation that transpired afterwards is encrypted to a nicety, because we know that passwords are a dead letter.

You see, one day, our cluster got so big that we could factor every single password that a human being could remember–every phrase, every nonsense string, up to 1,000 characters. Now, somewhere out there is a memnist freak or stage performer who can do better than that, but he probably doesn't have any secrets worth keeping.

Getting the Shithouse to that scale required discipline. At a certain point, we needed to actually go around and pull the plug on a lot of old-school gear, rescind our all-comers-welcome policy. We replaced it with a four-cores-or-go-home rule, and then bumped that to six cores, then eight. It didn't matter: out in the real world of retail hardware, they were shoving cores into cheapass consumer hardware so fast that we could afford to monotonically raise the bar for donations and still never run short.

We ran it against the salts used for well-known WiFi routers and produced tables that we uploaded to cheap cloud storage, clearing the hard-drives for the next round–password hashes for major OSes, hashes for embedded systems, photocopiers, keyless entry door-locks . . . Theoretically, the manufacturers could have made these much stronger but they weren't thinking ahead to the day when three weirdos might build themselves a cluster that could grind ceaselessly through the whole universe of "a" to

"zzzzzzzzzzzzzzzzzzzzzzzzzzzzzzzzzzzzzzzzzzzzzzzzzzzzzzzzzzzzzzzzzzzzzzzzzzzzzzzzzzzzzzzz
zzzzzzzzzzzzzzzzzzzzzzzzzzzzzzzzzzzzzzzzzzzzzzzzzzzzzzzzzzzzzzzzzzzzzzzzzzzzzzzzzzzzzzz
zzzzzzzzzzzzzzzzzzzzzzzzzzzzzzzzzzzzzzzzzzzzzzzzzzzzzzzzzzzzzzzzzzzzzzzzzzzzzzzzzzzzzzzz
zzzzzzzzzzzzzzzzzzzzzzzzzzzzzzzzzzzzzzzzzzzzzzzzzzzzzzzzzzzzzzzzzzzzzzzzzzzzzzzzzzzzzzzz
zzzzzzzzzzzzzzzzzzzzzzzzzzzzzzzzzzzzzzzzzzzzzzzzzzzzzzzzzzzzzzzzzzzzzzzzzzzzzzzzzzzzzzz
zzzzzzzzzzzzzzzzzzzzzzzzzzzzzzzzzzzzzzzzzzzzzzzzzzzzzzzzzzzzzzzzzzzzzzzzzzzzzzzzzzzzzzz
zzzzzzzzzzzzzzzzzzzzzzzzzzzzzzzzzzzzzzzzzzzzzzzzzzzzzzzzzzzzzzzzzzzzzzzzzzzzzzzzzzzzzzzz
zzzzzzzzzzzzzzzzzzzzzzzzzzzzzzzzzzzzzzzzzzzzzzzzzzzzzzzzzzzzzzzzzzzzzzzzzzzzzzzzzzzzzzzz
zzzzzzzzzzzzzzzzzzzzzzzzzzzzzzzzzzzzzzzzzzzzzzzzzzzzzzzzzzzzzzzzzzzzzzzzzzzzzzzzzzzzzzz
zzzzzzzzzzzzzzzzzzzzzzzzzzzzzzzzzzzzzzzzzzzzzzzzzzzzzzzzzzzzzzzzzzzzzzzzzzzzzzzzzzzzzzz

zzzzzzzzzzzzzzzzzzzzzzzzzzzzzzzzzzzzzzzzzzzzzzzzzzzzzzzzzzzzzzzzzzzzzzzzzzzzzzzzzzzzzzzzzz
zzzzzzzzzzzzzzzzzzzzzzzzzzzzzzzzzzzzzzzzzzzzzzzzzzzzzzzzzzzzzzzzzzzzzzzzzzzzzzzzzzzzzzzzzz
zzzzzzzzzzzzzzzzzzzzzzzzzzzzzzzzzzzzzzzzzzzzzzzzzzzzzzzzzzzz."

And after a while, the cluster got big enough to recompute against any new salt in pretty short time, especially with our information about the most-common passwords. We were pretty self-congratulatory, I must admit–very proud to have out-thought all those silly engineers and product managers.

Of course, none of *us* had the foresight to imagine that the day was coming when you could replicate our work for $12 worth of time on a cheesy cloud host in Bulgaria or some other exotic place. No, we were too busy forming an order of knights.

"Knighthood?" Tracey and Tristan looked at me like I was insane.

I felt my chin jut out at a belligerent angle and I reeled it back in. "It's either that or a league of super-heroes. Look, with great power comes great responsibility. We need a moral compass to ensure that we use our powers for good. We need chivalry, a code. Now, superheroes are cool and all, but the 'Justice League of the Rainbow Table' isn't nearly so cool as 'Knights of the Rainbow Table,' is it?"

We'd been building up these enormous tables, and theoretically, we hadn't touched them except to try them out on our own tame little testfiles. The reality was much more sordid, of course. I'd made a project of cracking the WPA passwords for at least two routers in every place I frequented, so that I could use them as I roamed the city. And once I was on them, well, it was only natural that my curiosity would compel me to have a sneaky-peeky at the traffic on the network, snaffle up some email and tweets and Facebook nonesuchs. Not that there was anything there worth looking at—I could play *Rear Window* all day and night and the most sordid thing I'd find was a little tax cheating, some unimaginative dirty talk, people losing their tempers at each other and snorting and steaming like Yosemite Sam without any capital letters or the benefit of spellcheck.

But I couldn't look away. At first, it was the horror of how naked it all was, the sheer volume of unencrypted credit card numbers, login credentials, and assorted Personally Identifying Information–PII, the smog of the 21st century, ubiquitous and impossible to be rid of.

Even after the shock of other people's technologically naive vulnerability wore off, I *still* looked, because I couldn't look away. I'm a monkey, I'm descended from monkeys, and the monkeys I'm descended from beat all the other monkeys by figuring out how to work together, and the secret to that is keeping track of all the other monkeys to make sure that they're not sleeping in a tree while you're gathering the fruit. I could not look away. If you could, well, you're a better monkey than me.

"Me too," Tracey admitted. "The kids next door are really creatively vicious about some other kid at school, a girl who picked on them who they've been quietly sabotaging for weeks now. Lots of fake social network stuff, imaginary boyfriends asking her to send topless photos, the whole lot. It's like a car-crash with a side of child porn, so icky but I bet you can't eat just one."

Tristan blushed and looked down and looked up and looked down. "My neighbor's got a bunch of IP-enabled CCTVs in his house and he picks his nose and I can't look away."

"Look, it's not the locks that keep you from breaking into your neighbor's house, right? I mean, any of us could figure out how to pick a lock in about a day, right? It's ethics. Social contract. It's a belief in the nobility of doing right and being good and doing unto others and all that. A million daycare workers who told you to share your toys, no punching, don't eat off that other kid's plate." I'd been up all night tossing and turning about this, in between watching an insomniac somewhere on my block get into a vicious Wikipedia edit-war over the history of Glock semi-automatics with an intensity that made me suspect he had a basement full of the things and had spent a lot of time contemplating what he might do with them.

"What I'm saying is, here we have all this power and if we want to be a force for good, well, that won't happen automagically. We're going to have to do something, something substantial and you know, formal if we're going to steer clear of being creepy evil voyeurs."

"Creepy evil voyeurs?" Tristan said.

"It's a term of art," I said.

"Yeah, the peril of CEV beckons," Tracey said.

"So why not a knighthood? After all, isn't that what knights were all about? We've got swords and armor and training and we could theoretically go around beheading and disemboweling willy nilly, but instead we'll develop some sort of formal code that we'll all abide by that specifies exactly whose head we're going to remove and whose bowels we're going to dis."

"What's wrong with not disemboweling altogether?" Tristan said. He was a pacifist at heart.

Tracey crossed her eyes at him. "You're joking, right? Once you've got swords, you can't *not* have swords. Are you going to take apart the Shithouse?"

Just the thought of it made my neck and shoulders tighten up like a tennis racket. "No one's going to shut down the cluster."

"Course not," Tristan said. He looked even more scandalized than me by the thought.

The day we took the Shithouse apart was one of those unexpected sunny, dry days that reminded you that the Bay Area was in fact part of California and not a distant satellite of some gloomy, rain-drenched place up in Oregon or Washington. All it took was one tiny whisper of a police investigation to cause the university administration to suddenly remember that they owned the Shithouse and had been paying our increasingly substantial electric bills for a decade. It had been so long since we'd seen anyone who wasn't one of our overworked free undergrads at the Shithouse that none of us really knew what to make of the campus security people who strutted into the Shithouse office. Lady Tracey was napping on the couch and I was playing a German board-game with Sir Tristan, and we all roused ourselves and looked up when the door opened and admitted five boxy guys in boxy coats with boxy utility belts and boxy walkie-talkies. My first thought was, "It's been years since we cracked the password on those walkie-talkies, why haven't we been listening in on them?"

Actually, that was like, my third thought. My first thought was, "Who are those guys?" and my second thought was, "Oh crap, we are so hosed."

"Can I help you gentlemen?"

"You're going to have to leave," said one, an older guy who seemed to be in charge. He had a close-cropped horseshoe-fringe of grey hair and his campus security jacket was threadbare and shiny at the elbows, but he had a personal presence that asserted itself and made it clear to all of us that he was the boss and expected to be obeyed. I guess he'd been at it for a while.

"Is there something on fire or something?" Tristan said.

The old guy cocked his head at Tristan, seemed to get the measure of him straight off. I guess he'd been working campus security long enough to recognize Tristan's species of spacy otherworldliness as genuine.

"No, son," he said with near-gentleness. "You're no longer allowed to use this facility. We're shutting it down."

"You can't do that," said Tracey.

"Ma'am," the old guy said. His badge said N. STRUBE. "Ma'am, I've been asked by the dean's office to close this place down and remove every person

I find from its premises. I've been asked to remove you, in other words. But I haven't been asked to take you into custody or even take down your name. That's a curious thing, isn't it? Almost like they don't want to have to admit that they knew what was going on in this place. Are you taking my meaning?"

Tracey nodded. "Perfectly," she said. Perfectly–as in perfectly composed, which she was and I wasn't. "But I don't think you understand mine: if you shut down the cooling system before you shut down those computers, the temperature in this building is going to hit 160 degrees Fahrenheit in about five minutes flat. If you're lucky, the computers will burn out then, but my guess is that a large number of them will be on fire before that happens."

It was right, of course, but I couldn't believe Tracey was saying it so calmly. She must have rehearsed this scene in her head. We all knew that there was a chance we'd get caught some day, but when I considered that possibility, I jerked my mind away from it as though I'd grazed a raw nerve. So Tracey was acting out some longstanding nightmare scenario, just as in charge as Mr. N. STRUBE. He seemed to recognize it.

"That's a very interesting fact, young woman," he said. "It wouldn't happen to be one of those very convenient facts that you just happened to have to hand for a situation like this, would it?"

Tracey cocked her head. "Sir, I'm not nearly that cunning." She was, in fact, lots more cunning. "But hey, these computers started out as trash, they're probably headed back into the trash after this, so I guess there's no reason not to incinerate them. But it seems unnecessarily messy, if you take my meaning."

"I don't suppose you have an alternative?" He was trying to keep a small smile off his face. He wasn't trying very hard. Authority figures loved Tracey when she was doing her little mischievous scamp thing.

"Well, I was thinking we could go around and power them all down clean, take them apart, make it possible to salvage as much as we can." She shrugged. "I guess it's probably university property in some sense or another." She shrugged again. "Your call."

But she had already moved to a keyboard, started to login–she had an improbably long password, we all did, for obvious reasons–and shut them all down.

N. STRUBE cleared his throat. "What, exactly, are you doing?"

"Shutting things down," she said.

"I thought you said it was my call."

She gave him a look that was one part good-natured ribbing, one part withering scorn. "Seriously? OK then, you make the call."

He stopped trying to hide his smile. "Yeah, all right, shut it down, take it apart, whatever it is you do."

I wanted to call up some of our undergrad slaveys and put them to work unpulling the cables, disconnecting the power-supplies, bringing down the hinky, freaky cooling system clean. But Tracey told me not to be a simp and pointed out that this was all on the d-l, a tacit understanding between her and the forces of N. STRUBE, and that bringing in a bunch of bigmouthed frosh would clobber all that.

So we did it ourselves. First, Tracey sent out a broadcast command to all the servers to begin erasing their hard drives, starting by nuking the catalog file on the data-partition and then going to work on zeroing out all the sectors with multiple passes, a process that could take a very long time. We didn't have a very long time, of course, but: "It won't hurt. Just start yanking the power cables and bundling them up and rolling up the network cables. Stack the machines out on the loading bay and take your time, so we zero out as many sectors as possible. Anything to screw up the forensics." N. STRUBE pointedly pretended that he didn't hear this.

It was dusty, hot work. The computers' fans had sucked all the brick-dust and pigeon guano and skin cells that had sifted down through the Shithouse's high rafters and spat it out along the backs of the shelving, mixing with the moisture in the air to form a gunky crust that stuck to our hands and clothes and got in our mouths and up our noses. But as unpleasant as that was, it wasn't nearly so terrible as the realization–which washed over me every minute or two–that we were done for.

There came a point when nearly all of the machines had been terminated, gutted and stacked, hundreds of them in sloppy, teetery towers on the loading bay floor. N. STRUBE had been examining our cooling system carefully, and he broke off to meander over to Tracey. I joined them. Tristan kept coiling up Ethernet cable. "It seems to me that we could take it from here. Nothing's going to burst into fire at this stage, right?"

Tracey shrugged. "I suppose not."

"And that big red shut-off button for the cooling system, that'll do it, yeah?" Another shrug.

"Well, then, I expect that you'd better be off. We can take it from here."

Tracey nodded, defeated. "We've got some personal things up in the office." Some personal things? For years, we'd been dumping everything that didn't fit our crackerbox apartments into the office–everything from old sofas to Tristan's obsessive German board-game collection.

"Well, gather up what you can carry then, and clear out."

"You've been very kind about this," Tracey said. The hard physical labor had baked out all her mischief and wrung out all her fortitude, leaving her small and tired.

Now, Sir Tristan, on the other hand–it was like he'd absorbed every erg of energy that Lady Tracey had lost. It was the thought of abandoning his German board-game collection, I think. It gave him the strength of 10 men, like a mother lifting a 16-wheeler off her baby. He used Ethernet cables to make huge bundles of the games, four of them, each ten feet high, and ferried them down the stairs from the foreman's office to the front door in four trips.

"Now what?" Tracey said. "I'm not carrying those things."

Tristan shook his head. "Just help me load up." He bent double, hand braced on his knees, back flat. "Stick 'em on in order."

He'd left long yokes of category-5 enhanced cable dangling off the game-bundles. The nearest bundle was the tallest, but had the shortest yoke. I heaved it up onto his skinny back and threaded the cables over his shoulders, helping him get his fingers twined in them. The next pile of games was a little shorter, but with a longer yoke, long enough to reach past the bottom bundle and get into his fingers. The third pile was smaller, with a longer yoke still, but by the time I had it piled on his back, his knees were trembling and he was making horrible little *unh unh* noises like he was about to split open.

"I'll get the last one, Tristan," I said. I hefted it onto my own back. It was the smallest of the four, but it was still so heavy that by the time I'd made it out to the main road, I was gasping and groaning. But Tristan was still moving, actually managing to lift and shuffle his feet along, each step coming with a chorus of grunts. When we got to the curb, he whimpered, "Get them off God get them off." I hastily set down my bundle, then began unloading him. I was reaching for the last stack when he collapsed forward, face first into the curb. I shoved the games off him and rolled him over. His face was streaming with blood from his nose and chin, which was split and filthy with gravel. He bucked and began to throw up, the vomit streaming down his cheeks and up his nose.

Knights don't surrender to squeam. I rolled him back over, helped him to his knees, pulled up his t-shirt and used it to wipe his face clear. He stank. I stank. We'd been moving computers all day, disturbing all that dust. I didn't even *like* Tristan very much at this stage. But we were both Knights of the Rainbow Table.

"How will we get all these home?" was the first intelligible thing he said.

"You're welcome," I said.

"I can't leave them here," he said.

Tracey caught up with us then. She'd been talking with N. STRUBE, squaring something away. "Thanks, guys. You managed to make the shittiest day of my life even shittier." Lady Tracey wasn't big on the chivalric code.

"Can I borrow your car?" I said. She was the only one of us with a car; in the Berkeley student circles we ran in, owning a car was only slightly less reprehensible than eating veal.

"Not if you're going to get fluids on it," she said.

Tristan looked up from his labors, tears and bile dripping off his sunken, stubbly cheeks. "I can walk," he said. "Just take the games."

He did walk. It turned out later that he'd partially herniated a disk, broken two ribs and torn up his intercostals muscles pretty badly. We saved all the games. They're still in my living room. I haven't used–I haven't *seen*—my sofa in six months.

###

Moszkowski sent us another email: "We need an expert. No one in a black t-shirt with vaguely threatening slogans a judge won't understand on it. Someone in a tie. Someone with a major university would be good. Your asses are on the line."

"I've got a crazy idea," I said to Tracey. We'd gone to her house to meet because my place was full of board games and Tristan was living in a residential hotel that averaged three tweeky meth-freaks per square yard. Tracey's run-down bungalow was in a crappy neighborhood and the water in the faucets ran brown and stank, but compared to us, she was the picture of middle-class respectability.

"Hit me," Tracey said. Tristan was staring out the window, seemingly oblivious, which either meant he had drifted off into the realm of pure thought, or he was listening intensely and not giving any outward sign of it.

"What if we ask Niratpattanasai?"

"Yeah, that's a stupid idea all right," Tracey said.

Niratpattanasai was the undoing of the Knights of the Rainbow Table. We'd happened upon his router on a reccy mission through the Outer Richmond, sniffing it with a clever little protocol analyzer that Tristan had bodged together. It could look at the way that a router broadcasted its ID and managed unsuccessful login attempts and make a highly accurate guess as to the make, model and firmware running on it. Every router had its idiosyncrasies, and Tristan had made a protracted assessment of these and loaded it onto his phone. Tristan's phone had begun its life as a slim and elegant example of the mobile designer's art, but he'd rubberbanded four external batteries and an ugly, solder-spotted antenna to it, so it looked more like an IED.

But it could spot an out-of-date router at 2,000 yards, snaffle up enough packets to get a lock on its encryption key, blast it through the rainbow tables, and have root access in five minutes flat. Tristan wore out three pairs of shoes a year, walking the streets of the greater Bay Area in search of misconfigured and out-of-date wireless networks. All that walking had melted off the few ounces of fat he'd started with and left him looking like a crosshatched anatomical drawing with a deep farmer's tan that was nut-brown below the sleeve mark and fishbelly pale above it. He had it set to vibrate and kept it in his front pocket, and he stalked the streets of San Francisco at a brisk pace, holding an ereader up to nose height and reading the day's papers. Sir Tristan read an average of forty daily newspapers a day. He was the 20 percent of readers who account for 80 percent of sales. Actually, he was the one percent of 20 percent who accounts for 80 percent of the sales to the 20 percent. For someone as otherworldly as an elf, Tristan knew an awful lot about current events.

On that day, he was plowing through the day's digital edition of the Singapore *Straits Times*, a paper that was closer to a comic-book than a news-source, being heavily censored by Singapore's fun-loving Ministry of Information. But Tristan read for quantity, not quality. His phone started to buzz as he was finishing a report on a wedding-ring expo at the International Convention and Exhibition Centre. He finished the article, tucked the ereader into his back pocket, pulled out his phone and checked the screen.

It had found a late-model Linksys router, running a two-generations-back version of the firmware–the firmware that it had shipped with, most likely. Most people never update their routers; it's one of the top vectors for serious, life-destroying pwnage. Tristan's phone had already cracked the password:

H*bq#(6BFEqdJsdxj`W3jlP\*u_a/Ln,VkW0NeSMxxW'mSxTEFh2J BK.40Dg2"erk}XS,[;d^Z/\*6P1B})$ı_Xd6Zı BSbt9pKFi&KC8mfu8ıo$ Y<QUxP=f:f{\:m1<:6Pip}i_T3?T0vO[{L$6QE"\*&&B[P=hH72",R\*y&n >oj}IEI$;pg$r1MFQ_jSSYq||hds]~!\!T$W_nCHkFMXgye7q`VfR'V^@ (B6kXY()7p29$,JQ?H0*-bVFcQg[!-XYD

256 characters of extremely pseudorandom gibberish, well beyond the capacity of all but the most obsessive human being to recite, remember, or manually enter. A damned good password, in other words, and not the sort of thing you'd expect to find on an out-of-date router, unless it had been set up

by a security conscious friend or relative (say, a visiting granddaughter) and then forgotten.

Not that it mattered–our tables ran four times as deep, 2^750 more complex. And Tristan had the latest-and-greatest version of the router firmware on his phone. It took about eight minutes for his phone to install the patch, reboot the router, and restore its configuration file, including that insane-o network key.

It was during that eight-minute period that VJ Niratpattanasai, a freelance security expert and sometimes columnist, noticed that his router was going screwy. He already had his own protocol analyzer on the network and it logged every detail of Tristan's session. Niratpattanasai used a webcam situated on the old TV antenna on his roof–installed, he said, to help participate in a songbird census years before–to capture some pretty high-rez pictures of Tristan as he stood in place, reading a report on shipping container losses in the *Straits-Times* while glancing at his phone's screen from time to time. From those grainy images, Niratpattanasai was able to run a reverse-lookup against one of the new snoopy sites that applied face-recognition to the photos on the web in order to make guesses about identity. Tristan wasn't hard to find: there'd been photos of him on the web going back to the time he was 14 and built his first homepage on Geocities. But all the recent photos of Tristan featured two other people: an angular-jawed woman with straight bangs and glowering eyes and a slightly pudgy, slightly bald guy who liked to wear high-tech giveaway golf shirts and loose-fit jeans with his Birkenstocks. That would be me. Our identities were easy enough to ascertain, too.

Tristan was long gone–he was updating the firmware on three routers in succession at a low-rise apartment building on the next street–but Niratpattanasai was still on the case. We didn't know it, but he was peeling our lives like onions. He was good at that.

Tracey was very careful about her activities: she didn't need to stalk the streets to find places to perform her good deeds. Instead, she ran network probes through a series of anonymizing proxies, looking for improperly updated server software–mostly content management systems that had fallen behind in their patching schedules. She'd exploit the vulnerabilities, harvest the password file, grab the administrative passwords, take over the machines, update their back-ends (and any ancillary software she found there) and nuke any malware that had been installed before she got there. She averaged a dozen machines a day, day in and day out, and never missed a day, not even when she caught some kind of awful flu that had her seeing cross-eyed and barfing up her lungs for a week.

Back-tracing Tracey required someone a lot more clued in than any of the admins whose machines she was fixing. But some had made half-hearted attempts at it, dead-ending at her blinds and false-fronts. These abortive attempts had been documented on various security message boards, and once or twice Tracey had out-clevered herself by weighing in on these discussions with false clues. She wasn't as subtle as she thought, and Niratpattanasai combined these with some clever guesses and some shrewd detective work to turn up some damning evidence that was thoroughly linked to Tracey in about a dozen ways.

And me? I was the stupidest of us all, really. I used my powers to penetrate wireless networks, snoop on their traffic, pluck weak passwords and poor security practices out of the electromagnetic spectrum, and then I would use throwaway webmail accounts to conduct impromptu security masterclasses with the sloppy, the misinformed, and the careless. "Teach a man to fish," was my thinking and, at any given time, I had about a dozen "students." I'd gotten good at approaching people about their security lapses but it was inevitable that some people freaked and blabbed all over their Facebooks and such about the weird stranger bent on teaching them to protect themselves on the intertubes. Niratpattanasai found them, too, put two and two together, and wrote a major expose about us for the Sunday *New York Times* magazine, snagging the cover.

They held the presses until noon on Saturday so that they could add in the quotes he got from us as the FBI swooped down on us while we were eating bagels and vegan schmear at a hippie place near Tristan's favorite game store. I say "swooped," but they were very civilized about it. After they'd stationed guards at the front and rear entrances, three officers came in, showed us their badges, read out the charges, and asked us to come quietly.

Niratpattanasai rode in the back of the police wagon with us and used his phone to record a forty-five minute interview as we fought traffic to the federal courthouse where we were to be booked and held for arraignment in a crowded and miserable holding cell with an odd assortment of losers, the luckless, and villains. I can barely remember the questions he asked us, and I've never brought myself to download the audio file he posted in his "reporter's notebook" special on nytimes.com. But he didn't use any of my quotes in the article, which probably means I was boring. Tristan got three quotes: "I don't understand. I fixed your router!" and "What kind of phone is that?" and "Is it running up-to-date firmware?"

Tracey got *eight* quotes, most of them what they used to call "unprintable," except the *Times* printed them, because when Tracey gets angry, she's like a thesaurus of profanity. It's practically poetry, and it's got educational value in a world of dull, unimaginative cursing.

I knew a lawyer, my freshman year roommate in fact, who'd made junior partner at one of those Silicon Valley firms that specializes in patent litigation, finance, and bailing out high-tech executives who've flown their Soviet surplus jets too close to city limits or mixed an unwise cocktail of high-performance cars, smart drugs, energy beverages and Humboldt County's stinkiest, stickiest ganja.

The Feebs had a cybercrime creep who confiscated all our electronics and such and spirited them away from us, but he turned out to have a heart, because he retrieved Albert's–my ex-roommate's–number for me from my phone. Of course, he made me tell him my password in order to unlock the phone. He also made me wait while he did some kind of whole-disk copy from the phone's memory to an external drive, just in case the password I gave him was an alternate one that zeroed out the phone's storage, which made me feel flattered (that he thought me capable of such subtlety and forethought) and embarrassed (that I hadn't thought of it). He seemed disappointed when he checksummed the phone's storage after the password had been entered and saw that unlocking it hadn't altered it. I shrugged and wrote down the phone number on my arm with the soft-tipped Sharpie that was the only kind of writing implement we were allowed to have.

Albert hadn't changed his cellular number in years–he was good like that– and he picked up on the third ring, sounding sleepy.

"Lo?"

Something about the quality of the line and the texture of the quiet said 'overseas hotel room.' "Where are you?"

"France." He blew his nose. "Haven't heard from you in a while."

I did the math in my head. 3PM here was, uh, 7AM there, on a Sunday. "I'm sorry to wake you up. I, well, is there someone you might recommend, a lawyer, for a federal Computer Fraud and Abuse arraignment?"

I heard him sit up, fumble with his glasses, a light switch. "Who's been charged?"

"Um," I said.

"You? You seemed like such a nice boy in school. Where are they holding you?"

I told him, and spelled Tracey and Tristan's names for him. "Do you have any money?"

"Not the kind that your firm charges," I said. I'd once recommended him to a client I was freelancing with and the client had called them up and then pointed out that they were proposing to charge more than his company's entire annual budget just to review a deal.

"We'll sort that out. But you'll need some assets or cash if you're going to make bail. Cars, houses, stocks? Your parents' house?"

"I'd hoped I wouldn't have to talk to my parents."

"You seriously think that having a difficult conversation with your parents is the worst thing that's going to happen to you at this stage?

Ouch. "Well put."

"Niratpattanasai did all those interviews and articles and TV appearances but he never once accused us of wrongdoing. He went to great pains to say that we were doing good."

Tracey skewered me on a very Tracey-ish glare. "He went to pains to say that we *believed* we were doing good. He also took pains to say that we were lawless vigilantes who had committed thousands of felonies."

Normally, I would have backed down to Tracey. We both did, most of the time. But ever since I stopped eating, I'd found new wellsprings of willpower, new bravery I'd never had before. "Moszkowski said we needed an expert who would testify that we'd acted without malicious intent. I think Niratpattanasai's got integrity, he'll say that if they ask him. And who could ask for a better expert? I mean, really!"

Tristan nodded. "I think he's right. Niratpattanasai would be great. I like him."

Tracey tried the eye-laser thing on Tristan but the beams just bounced off his impenetrable shield of weird. "You like him?"

"He did really good work tracking us down. It can't have been easy. For all he knew we were bad guys going around messing everything up. I think he could have been a Knight if we'd asked him early enough."

"You mean, before he got us arrested?"

"Yeah. Sir Niratpattanasai."

Tracey readied another volley but I put up my hand. "Look, forget the cut and thrust and *think*, Tracey. Whatever else Niratpattanasai is, he's not a liar or a fool. He may not understand or like what we did but, if someone puts him on the stand and asks if we were doing anything malicious, he'll tell the truth."

She balled up her hands into fists and took two deep breaths. Then she opened her hands. "Fine, that's no stupider than any of the ideas we've had so far and smarter than most of them." She hit the intercom button on the phone on the board-room table. "Can you please tell Mr. Moszkowski we'd like to speak to him?"

The law firm had given us use of one of its small boardrooms because we couldn't agree on any other meeting place–I couldn't abide restaurants (obviously), public places gave Tristan the heebie-jeebies, and Tracey couldn't stand to be in either of our apartments ("They smell like unwashed boy," she'd said, with characteristic candor) and she wouldn't have us in her place ("*You* smell like unwashed boy.")

Moszkowski listened patiently as we explained our thinking to him. "You can't call the prosecution's main witness in your defense," he said.

"Is that a law," Tristan said.

"It's not a law. It's just common sense."

"Oh, that," Tristan said. "We don't really do that."

"At last, something we all agree on," Tracey said.

"Yeah," I said. "Common sense is something that happens to other people. We're more about, you know, higher purposes and all that."

"And look how far that's got you," Moszkowski snapped. But I could tell that he was weakening. He'd done some showy, flashy things in his long and storied career and he clearly saw that this was going to be one for the scrapbook (assuming he could pull it off.)

All that remained was to call on Niratpattanasai.

Of course we knew where he lived. If Tristan hadn't found his house, none of this would have happened and we could have gone on breaking the law forever. Or at least, until someone else figured it out. Niratpattanasai wasn't the only smart person on the Internet.

"You knock," Tristan said. He didn't like touching other peoples' doors. Plus, we were all a little worried that Niratpattanasai'd answer the door with a shotgun or a crossbow or one of those huge two-handed Klingon disemboweling swords.

Tracey did her decisive thing and made a fist but I was already rapping at the door, tapping into that reserve of strength I'd found when most of my body melted away.

He answered the door in bare feet and jeans, his hair wet from the shower. He was wearing a t-shirt advertising a German board game called Elefanten-Parade, which I happened to know that Tristan worshipped. We'd played it a few times with Tracey and even she had to admit it was a pretty engrossing and clever bit of design, plus the wooden elephant tokens were really beautiful.

"That is such a great game," Tristan said, without preamble.

"Nice to see you, too," Niratpattanasai said. He was Thai, and a little short by American standards, about Tracey's height. He had friendly eyes and one of those faces that looked like it would seem very young until it suddenly seemed very old. "Um, you're not here to beat me up or anything, right?"

Tracey made a rude noise. Tristan asked him where he got his shirt. I held up my hands with their matchstick fingers and said, "We come in peace."

"You'd better come in, then," he said.

It was a nice place, but not crazy-nice, the home of a moderately well-off tech freelancer in San Francisco. There were framed photos of vintage computers in the hallway and a $5,000 coffee machine that looked like a brass Dalek in the kitchen (I know exactly what it costs, because I'd priced them myself just about every time I came into a little money, but it was never enough). He made us espressos, grinding the beans in a heavy, noisy burr grinder that looked like it had been to the wars. "I brought it to Burning Man," he said. "Getting the playa dust out meant totally disassembling it and then I lost part of the housing for a while and just used duct tape until I found it at the back of a cupboard. But it's a great machine."

The espresso was black as licorice and it sported a velvety cream that was sweet and bitter at once and everything I imagined that particular espresso machine would be if I could ever afford it. I was suddenly and immensely jealous of Niratpattanasai. We'd been off doing good deeds for years while he worked the private sector and pulled down enough money to buy really top-notch coffee gadgets. My life sucked.

It was about to get worse. "Can I use your toilet?" I said.

Niratpattanasai must have seen the alarm on my face because he almost sprinted up the stairs, me on his heels. I barely got through the door before the coffee came back up again, landing in the toilet bowl with a spatter. I'd had enough practice at puking that I hardly made any sound. Afterwards, I rinsed out my mouth with water from the faucet and dried my hands and face on a damp towel that hung from the shower rod. The bathmat was damp, too. I saw that he used the same shampoo that I used, a peppermint hippie brand that was certified to be organic, fair trade, phosphate-free, not tested on animals, and produced by a unionized workforce. I liked it because it smelled nice.

When I came back to the kitchen, Tracey looked at me with a mix of disgust and pity. Tristan was geeking out over a poster printed with a million-digit prime (in very small type). Niratpattanasai asked if I was OK.

"Yeah," I said. "It's fine. Just a thing."

Tracey said, "He can't eat anymore. Every time he tries, whoosh, up it comes."

"Have you been to the doctor?"

I wished Tracey hadn't said anything. I hated explaining this. "I've had a bunch of tests. Everyone's pretty convinced it's stress-related."

"He's crazy," Tracey said.

"Thanks, Tracey."

She rolled her eyes. "It's not like he couldn't figure that out for himself. So, are you going to do it, Niratpattanasai?"

"You already asked him?" I said.

"While you were in the john calling Europe on the porcelain telephone, yes."

I turned to Niratpattanasai. "So?"

"Look," he said. "I just don't know. To tell you the truth, I feel pretty bad about this. I mean, you guys—"

Tracey cleared her throat loudly.

"You *folks* seem like nice people. Weird, but nice. And I'm sorry about your, you know, health thing. But look at it from my perspective: from what I could tell, you guys had been running around, breaking into every damn kind of system there was, from home routers to big websites and installing arbitrary code. From what I could tell, you were a three-person crime-wave. I wanted to keep people safe—"

"But that's all we were doing," Tristan said, a petulant note in his voice.

"Yeah, I figured that out when I checksummed the firmware update you stuck on my router and saw that you'd been trying to help out. But it's creepy, you understand, right? What gives you the right to go around breaking into people's systems, even if you're just 'fixing' them? What if you patched something and broke something else in the process? What if you took some hospital's life-support system offline when you updated its router?"

"Oh, I usually mapped out the whole network and checked the patch-levels of everything inside it before I updated anything," Tracey said.

"So you mitigated the harm from breaking into peoples' systems by breaking into more systems? Nice one."

"We had a code," I said, heading off Tracey before she could get into an epic flamewar in Niratpattanasai's kitchen.

"A code," he said.

"A chivalric code."

"Great. You're LARPers." He drew himself up and then made a leg and bowed low over it. "Prithee, good knight, do telleth me of yon chivalric code, that I dost mightest come to a full understanding of thine good deeds."

Tristan laughed, an unexpected sound. "Dude that's terrible medieval dialog. 'Yon chivalric code?' 'Telleth?'"

"He was being sarcastic," Tracey said.

Tristan's eyes sparkled. "So was I," he said, and I suddenly remembered that in addition to being an otherworldly pain in the ass, Tristan Erkko was one of the smartest people I'd ever known. It was easy to forget. Some smart people are very stupid. Just look at me.

"Look," I said. "I know it sounds stupid, but look, it's no more stupid than any other law, rule or code you've ever heard of. It's just a social contract: we developed a great power, so we took responsibility for it."

"Spiderman," he said.

"That doesn't make it any less valid," I said. "What is it that stops you breaking into your neighbors' houses? You've got a sweet set of lockpicks on your keyring over there." I'd noticed it when we first came into the kitchen. They looked like they'd been handmade and well-finished, not a burr or a rough spot on them, and they were worn smooth from lots of handling. "Those Yale locks your neighbors use, you could go through 'em like a knife through butter. You work from home, most of them are out during the day. So when you run out of sugar or need a bit of milk, why don't you just let yourself into your neighbor's kitchen, help yourself and replace it when you get back? What's the harm?"

"It's wrong," he said. "It's an invasion of their privacy. I might scare someone. I'd hate it if someone did it to me."

"And it's illegal," Tracey said.

"That, too," he said.

"You notice how the law was the last thing on your list? How you left it off your list until Tracey reminded you? The law isn't what keeps us in check. Social codes, voluntary and largely unspoken are what keep us from cutting up our neighbors, taking their things, punching them when they cut us off on the freeway. But social codes take time, they don't automagically appear as soon as new technologies arrive. In the heat of the moment, sitting there with power your neighbors don't have, asking yourself whether using these new powers is ethical or unethical–well, it's pretty much guaranteed that you're going to choose the most self-serving, easy rationalization you can sneak past your own flinch reaction. Reading your neighbors' email isn't like opening their mail or holding a glass to their door, because, well, because their WiFi is in your living room, so it's like they're dangling their email on a clothesline at eye-height in front of your sofa.

"But we didn't try to formulate moral codes on the fly, when temptation was before us. We sat down and coldly, rationally decided what we would do in the future. We did it when we were comfortable and relaxed, we made an agreement, and we stuck to it."

"And what was this 'ethical code?'" Niratpattanasai said.

"First: To use our cluster only to detect vulnerable systems and machines. Second: To bring those systems into less-vulnerable states. Third: To retain no credentials that would allow us to regain access to the systems once they had been improved. Fourth: To work only in the service of improving systems, and to do nothing that wasn't part of that goal."

Niratpattanasai opened his mouth, then closed it and visibly thought about what I'd said. He drummed his fingers. "OK," he said. "That's not bad. But man, there's a lot of wiggle-room in there. There's a large amount of stuff that you could pry into on the way to making sure that something is secure."

"We rattled the doorknobs to make sure they were locked, and when we found unlocked ones, we locked them," I said.

"OK, but did you try the windows and the chimneys, too? Did you snip the burglar alarm wires to see if it could be shut down with a pair of pliers?"

"There's no security in obscurity," I said. "We tried to fix every vulnerability we could imagine, because bad guys would try to attack every vulnerability they could imagine. Why should we do any less?"

"Is that the same as saying there aren't any loopholes in your little chivalric code?"

I shrugged. "No. It's not an algorithm, it's a heuristic. It's meant to be interpreted by good people who want to do good and are of good will and good faith."

"Goodness gracious," he said.

I shrugged again. "It comes down to this: you saw the work we did. Now, either we spent most of our time going around making the world a safer, more secure place, or that was all an elaborate cover for some kind of leet haxor thing where we were really pwning all these boxes to rip people off and spy on them."

"Those are the only two possibilities? What about the possibility that you were imperfectly chivalric? Maybe you had this code that said you'd stay on the up and up while you were spelunking through private, sensitive systems and maybe you *also* sometimes slipped up and got a peek at peoples' secrets and private lives and looked a little longer than you could possibly justify."

Whatever is the opposite of a poker face, that's what I have. Of course I had. I wasn't proud of it, and I hadn't done anything with it but, when you discover that someone sweet and lovable is privately trash-talking his sainted mother or having cybersex with a life-insurance salesman in Norway, it's impossible not to look. Like a car crash.

"Aha," he said.

"Never voluntarily, never for long, and never to anyone's detriment."

"You sound like you've practiced that."

He was really, really smart, in that annoying way of people who notice exactly the thing you hope they won't notice. I felt the shame burn in the tips of my ears. "You've got me. But we never set out to be anything except a force for good."

"Every vigilante could say the same thing."

There it was, the v-word, the one we avoided even amongst ourselves. "Vigilantes go after bad guys, we helped innocent people defend themselves. We never strung anyone up."

"No matter how guilty they were," Tracey said.

"It's a fine distinction."

"But it's a distinctive one," I said.

He nodded thoughtfully. Tracey and Tristan stared at me with a mixture of fear and surprise. I was once the persuader of our little group but I hadn't been doing much talking lately.

"What the hell," Niratpattanasai said. "I suppose it is at that. Yeah, fine. You've got yourself a witness for the defense. But I'm going to tell the truth, the whole truth and so forth. Even the embarrassing parts. You seem like essentially nice people and I can't really say I believe that my tax dollars should be spent on imprisoning you."

I managed some dry toast and a smoothie with bodybuilder powder that night, which was a banquet by my standards.

I've had a little online presence since the gofer days, just an ugly, mostly text vanity page with links to some stuff I'd made or done or admired. It ran on a thin little webserver that had all of 85 lines of code, and I kept it all religiously patched. Of course I used a secure password for it, 256 pseudorandom characters that I kept stashed–along with all my other passwords—in a file that I kept on a thumb drive and on a remote server. The file itself was encrypted to the longest password I could remember, a mnemonic derived from a deck of shuffled cards that I'd memorized using a technique I found online and practiced for two months before I had it down cold. My 52-character password (one character each for value) wasn't the sort of thing that you expect anyone to break, which is why I felt OK about downloading the file over untrusted networks even though someone might have sniffed it as it came down to me.

But of course, I wasn't the only guy in the world with a cluster. Anyone and everyone could rent an unimaginable amount of compute time for rock-bottom prices these days, the result of Moore's Law and relentless competition. Cracking my little 52-character password was probably the easy part. The hard part, of course, would have been arranging to be on a network from which I downloaded my file.

As it turned out, that part wasn't too hard. The denial-of-service attack on my site hit just as I was headed into Moszkowski's office for our weekly meeting. It took me about ten minutes to notice my mail-server (on the same machine) wasn't working, and then, of course, I downloaded the password file. Whatever hacker or group of hackers or spook decided to get me, they knew their stuff. Must have cracked the law office's wireless password well in advance, and it wasn't like that part of San Francisco lacked for inconspicuous spots where you could sit with a laptop that was snaffling up all the wireless traffic and decrypting it. Having snagged my password file, it wouldn't have taken much to take it to pieces, and then the bad guys could get into my bank, could sign legal documents on my behalf, could read my online archives, could do anything and everything they wanted with my mail and my web-server and whatever you want. That file was *me*, as far as the digital world was concerned, and it wasn't like there was much of a distinction between the real world and the digital one these days.

I pieced this together after the headlines, naturally. The email dump came simultaneous with the first news-story, and I'm pretty sure that the reporter—an online site infamous for its grabby headlines—had done a deal to get first crack at the messages. But I couldn't prove anything.

It's not like there was much that was that damning in the mail dump, of course. Tracey and I had traded some uncomplimentary emails about Tristan, but Tristan already knew he pissed us off all the time. And Tristan and I had been pretty crude in our discussion of the cluelessness of the security procedures at Moszkowski's office, which was a ho-ho-the-irony-it-burns moment good for a million pageviews.

Mostly, though, the public were interested in WHITE HAT HACKER CONSIDERED HIMSELF A KNIGHT CRUSADER and similar headlines and all the business where we'd hashed out the chivalric code. We had planned on downplaying the knight stuff while making sure the judge knew that we were only trying to help. Tristan liked to use renfaire speak in his emails on the subject, which made for great comedy moments, and even a bunch of meme-y photos of Tristan walking the streets of San Francisco, holding up his ereader, brow furrowed, eyes nested in a hashwork of squint-wrinkles. He'd already been a legendary San Francisco character ("The Ebook Walker," they called him, and put him in the pantheon that included Emperor Norton and Frank Chu and all the other street-nuts who'd made San Francisco great)–the news that he was also a member of the Knights of the Rainbow Table made for great captioning opportunities: FORSOOTH, I DOTH BE IN THINE NETWORK, PATCHING THINE FIRMWARE.

One thing I never did figure out: the person or people who pwned my webserver replaced my homepage with a picture of me from my fat days and a bunch of crude fat jokes. Meanwhile, they pulled off a hack that put a page they controlled into about ten million browsers over 24 hours. Couldn't they come up with anything more interesting to say to that many people? Hell, they could have just stuck some crappy ads on the page and made a couple thousand dollars, assuming they had the nous to put together an untraceable bank account for the money to land in. But my nemesis or nemeses apparently had nothing much to say to the world, only that I'd once been a "fat fuck." People are weird, their motives unknowable. This is a problem.

I had to pay a couple hundred bucks in hosting fees for all the traffic the hack generated, which was a kind of injury-to-insult moment, but given that I had already borrowed an entire mortgage's worth of money from my parents for our defense, I hardly felt the additional debt. But the email dump and the ensuing bad feelings from Tracey and Tristan made my life appreciably worse. Even though we'd stopped being anything like pals years before we'd been busted, we'd been comrades at least. Now we could barely stand to be in the same room together.

The email dump was a godsend to all the borderline personality types who assumed that anyone who tried to do something for good must be broken or awful or crazy. People who already hated us with the white-hot heat of a thousand suns pored over every line in a million emails stretching back to my high-school days (I have never knowingly deleted a non-spam message), mining them for the most embarrassing nuggets they could find. Like I said, there was nothing damning–nothing criminal, nothing a judge would care about–in there, but there was plenty that I never expected to have stuck in a tarball and torrented to a million bilious Internet trolls to laugh at.

But what got Moszkowski was that they leaked the fact that Niratpattanasai had agreed to testify on our behalf. He'd kept that as his ace in the hole and had planned out a whole dramatic revelation that would maximize his effect on the jury. Now that plan was blown and Moszkowski swore that the DA would be riding Niratpattanasai like a rodeo bull to get him to back out.

"I thought you were Mr. Security Guy," he said, finally, after a good twenty-minute rant about all the various and sundry ways in which our case was thoroughly, totally hosed.

"I am."

"So how the hell did this happen?"

I shrugged. "It happened because someone was determined enough to make it happen. Look, what we did was go around and look for stuff with obvious vulnerabilities that could be exploited at little or no cost, usually by automated attackers. But what happened to me—that was the work of someone really dedicated. What us Mr. Security Guys call an Advanced Persistent Threat. These used to be governments or major crime syndicates but, these days, all it takes to be an APT is to have a really intense bug up your ass, some spare time, and the ability to use a search engine and follow a recipe. The gap between APTs and automated, opportunistic attacks is narrowing. Give it a few years and it'll cease to exist altogether."

Moszkowski looked at me with his basset hound stare, the litigator's zero-emotion poker-face. "I'm pretty sure I understand what you just said and it scares the shit out of me."

I nodded. "Me too. It's not like it was hard to predict, either. It's been on the way for years. Look, we built our cluster out of garbage, but Moore's law means that by the time you've finished building your cluster out of free junk, you'll be able to buy the same amount of computation in factory packaging for about what your junk-cluster cost."

"So you saw this coming, huh?"

"In a way," I said. "Hence all the chivalric code stuff."

"But in another way, no," Tracey said. "None of us really wanted to confront what it means if passwords stop working."

"Wait, what? Passwords stop working?"

Tracey and Tristan and I shared a look. It was hard to remember, sometimes, that we lived and breathed something that other people thought of as esoteric and bizarre. It was like being a pathologist who saw little life-shortening labels attached to every hazard, while others tripped blithely past them, shoveling poison into their mouths, endangering their lives with vehicles and sex and sports and recreational chemicals. For a moment, I had a sense of what Moszkowski must be feeling, a vertiginous dropping-away of the safe crust over his world, revealing the yawning pit below.

"Not all of them. You can comfortably password-protect your hard-drive for quite some time–maybe forever. But for anything that lives on a network, anything that can be analyzed in private without shutting down after too many bad password attempts, well, I think we can safely declare them dead."

"I don't understand–which passwords are dead?"

"Pretty much anything other people can access. Wireless networks. A lot of stuff you do on wired networks, too. Any file you leave out there in the wild world, counting on a password to protect it."

"Is that all?" he asked. I'm pretty sure he was being sarcastic.

"Pretty much," I said. "I mean, give it a while. The future is here, it's just not evenly distributed, like the prophet O'Reilly said."

"He was quoting Gibson," Tristan said.

"Pedant," I said.

Moszkowski fisted at his tired, baggy eyes. "Just don't talk about this stuff in front of the judge, OK?"

"Why not?" I'd actually been thinking about how to frame it all. I mean, now that we were sure to be asked about the Knights and the code, I wanted to make sure that everybody understood that beneath all the play-acting there'd been a serious point that was going to affect them all.

"This apocalyptic talk, it's going to make you look like a nut."

The three of us looked at each other and then at our lawyer. "Which part of that was apocalyptic?" Tracey said.

"The part about passwords becoming useless," he said, as though he thought she was being sarcastic.

"Hal," she said, "everybody knows that."

"What do you mean, everybody? Our IT person still assigns passwords to our networks. She's not an idiot. So, does she know this?"

"Yes," Tracey said. "If she's not an idiot, she knows this."

"So why does she bother?"

"Well, because for now, it's enough to stop most automated attacks and they're in a different threat category to your APTs. APTs, they're like ninjas who can pick any lock and sneak into any house. But there's not a lot of ninjas, and they're expensive, so you either have to piss off a ninja or someone rich enough to hire a ninja, otherwise you're OK. We pissed off a ninja, which is surprisingly easy to do, because setting out to become a ninja is a kind of mentally unbalanced undertaking—"

"Not like setting out to be a knight," I said, quietly. Tracey gave me the finger without dropping a syllable.

"While automated attacks are like, well, like if the guy who smashed your car window and stole your GPS could do it again, in perfect stealth, from anywhere in the world. Or if *all* the guys who *might* smash your car window and steal your stereo could reach you, all at once. It's worth defending against those guys.

"But give it another couple years and those guys will be able to do most of the stuff a ninja can do, at least when it comes to passwords. They'll be able to replace expensive computers with cheap computers. They'll be able to replace cleverness with cheap computers. And there'll be a lot of cheap computers."

"So give it a couple years—"

"For the future to get evenly distributed," I said.

"And—"

"And?"

"What do we do then? How do we protect ourselves?"

"Dude, if we knew that, we'd be billionaires," I said.

"No, you wouldn't," Tracey said. "You'd be making someone else a billionaire. Some investor who bankrolled you and then ripped you off and kicked you out of your own company."

"No way," I said. "I'd totally have a great lawyer to help me like Hal here."

Hal shook his head. "She's right. You'd lose your shirt. Fine, it's not your fault, we're all going to hell in a handbasket, security is dead, the future isn't evenly distributed. Have I missed anything?"

"Well, there's the fact that whoever snaffled up my password file could have been watching your web-traffic and reading your email—that's why we kept nagging you to start using GPG."

He groaned. "I had a training session on it booked for next week."

Tracey patted his hand. "It's OK, everyone sucks at security."

A funny thing about having your secrets all exposed in one big whack: it's over quickly. I may have had a hobby that was as weird as a two headed snake but, apart from that, I was a monumentally boring individual. It pains me to admit it but it I was essentially a harmless kook.

The world took a hard run at my email corpus and pretty quickly extracted any messages having to do with sex, finances, or where I called someone a nasty name. Everyone had a good chuckle over these and then returned to their regularly scheduled porn, political arguments, and operating system advocacy.

Just like that, I was a nobody again. I took advantage of the lull to refurb an old computer and slap in a big hard-drive and download anything I'd stuck in the cloud to my local storage, wiping it all out behind me as thoroughly as I could. Most importantly, I stuck my master password file on the disk and not on the network, even though that meant I now had to concern myself with keeping backups separate from my machine. Moszkowski was good about letting me stick a drive in his desk drawer and back up to it every time I went by the law office. Every bit on it was encrypted with a new 52-character password that I memorized from a freshly shuffled deck of cards.

This may be the only positive aspect of being bankrupt and facing a jail sentence: I didn't really care about all those lost online accounts and I didn't really care that any loser could authenticate himself to my bank and pose as me and raid my empty bank accounts.

But I *did* feel a kind of hollowness that was even worse than the hunger that gnawed at my guts all day and all night. A feeling that I'd lost something, like I'd misplaced an internal organ. It wasn't something I could talk about with Tracey and Tristan–after all, a substantial portion of their email had been exposed along with mine, since I'd saved all the email they'd ever sent to me. Moszkowski would have lent a sympathetic ear but he wasn't really a member of my subspecies and there was some stuff we couldn't discuss.

There was really only one person I knew who was still on speaking terms with me. Unfortunately, he was the guy who'd gotten me in trouble in the first place.

###

Niratpattanasai answered his mobile phone on the third ring. "What can I do for you?" He knew who it was, I was already in his contacts database. He was that kind of organized.

"Where are you?"

"Why do you want to know?"

"Because I'm at your house and I've been ringing the doorbell for ten minutes and you haven't answered, so I'm assuming you're not home and hoping you're not too far away."

"Oh," he said. "OK, fine. You know, some people call *before* they come over. It's often considered the polite thing to do."

"So, are you far away?"

"I'm in the back yard," he said. "Can't hear the bell. Come around."

I found him standing over a large, gleaming gas barbeque fitted out with two propane bottles. He was working a hand-cranked coffee roaster with a large, battered scorched drum, wearing old clothes and a broad-brimmed, fraying straw hat. The smell was bitter but not unpleasant.

"You roast your own?"

"I'm learning," he said. "I've been practicing for a couple years now but I still can't get the hang of it. Trying to get a bean that's as good as the stuff the Australian cafe down the road sells." He shrugged. "I wish I could say that my beans taste better because I've roasted them myself, but I'd be lying. I'm an amateur and the lady who roasts for Cobbers does a new batch every week." He turned the crank for a while longer. "I'm getting better, though."

"The coffee you served me the other day was amazing."

"I cheated," he said. "It wasn't my roast." He turned a while longer. "And you vommed it up about ten seconds later."

"Ah," I said. "Nothing personal. Just a thing I do."

"So I gathered. I think that Tracey's right, you need to go back to the doctor about that."

She'd sent several pointed emails on the subject. "You had a look at the corpus, then?" Calling it "the corpus" helped me distance myself, damped down the visceral reaction I had whenever I thought about all that mail sitting there online.

"Couldn't help myself. Wish I'd signed up for your chivalric code, I might have been able to stop myself from peeking."

"You'd be the only one," I said.

He turned some more. "Well, it's bound to happen to lots more people soon enough. 'Course, you know that better than most people. No one can plug all the holes. It's like trying to stop burglars all by yourself, with bars and locks, instead of cops and social norms. Eventually you find yourself living in an armed compound, or losing everything. Look at me with my out-of-date firmware on my router."

"Nobody's perfect," I said.

We stood in silence for a time. He checked a timer stuck to the barbeque and stopped turning, killing the propane. He slipped on some oven mitts and did some after-roast arcana with tongs and bags and funnels. The smells were incredible. He piled his working instruments up on a picnic table and took off his gloves.

"Sucks about your email. How'd they get you?"

I told him what I'd guessed. He nodded. "Yeah, that would have gotten me too. You memorized a 50-character password?"

"52. Took some doing," I said. "But you could learn how to do it."

"Look, I've been in tech a long time, but I prefer to learn my skills at least ten minutes before they go obsolete."

"Good policy."

"So I guess that's it, huh? RIP, privacy, just like the Google Man said back in the old days. Christ, what an asshole."

"Oh, this is bigger than privacy. RIP, remote authentication is more like it. Or lots of kinds of remote auth. Passwords, anyway."

"Good riddance. Now I can free up all that disk space in my brain I've been devoting to storing and retrieving meaningless strings."

He led me inside and made some coffee for himself and got a glass of water for me. We sat down on his overstuffed, cat-hair-strewn embroidered sofa and sipped.

"Think you'll go to jail?"

"Don't feel guilty," I said. "If it wasn't you, it would have been someone else."

"I don't feel guilty," he said. "You had it coming. Chivalry or no, it's just creepy-wrong to let yourself into other peoples' computers and networks and poke around. If your point was to create a social norm of not breaking into other peoples' computers, maybe you could have tried *not breaking into other peoples' computers*. It's crazy, I know."

I hung my head. "Well, yeah," I said. "We could have done that."

"I should probably be angry at you," he said. "You know that there's going to be a million kids out there who try to copy what you did and justify it by saying that you did it."

"Well, not after they make an example of me and throw away the key."

"So you *do* think you're going to jail."

"Let's just say that my lawyer's advised me to think seriously about a 5-15 year hiatus from my career."

"Rough," he said. "How about your, uh, health issue?"

"Yeah," I said. "Well, it came on suddenly, maybe it'll go as quickly."

"You've had everything tested?"

I tapped my temple. "All in my head. Had every test you can name. I had good insurance. Anyway, maybe I'll memorize a few more pointless passwords and crowd it out of my brain. Always wanted to lose a couple pounds. Saving loads of money on food." I stopped. I could go on in that vein for a good ten minutes. "Sorry, I'm weirding you out."

"A little."

"Well, change of subject then. Do you think I could ask you something?"

"Based on all available evidence, I believe the answer is yes."

"That's a very Tristan sort of answer. He's a little frustrating but the neurotypical are so . . . boring. So look, the thing is, you got angry at us for doing what we did, which is fair enough. But that was about the whole *package*, right? It wasn't personal, it wasn't because Tristan fixed your router, right? I mean, you know he didn't look around when he was in, right? He was reading the *Irish Times*. It's a thing he does."

He got a guarded look. "Why are you asking this? I agreed to testify for you, I'd think that'd be all the reassurance you needed."

I spat it out before I could stop myself: "I just want to know if this feeling, this, you know, this *violated* feeling, if it's just me being a wimp or what? Do you think it'll go away? Did you feel it?"

"Oh, that. Huh. Well, in some ways, you're just feeling what every celebrity feels when the tabloids get hold of their voicemail. But, of course, there's a lot more than voicemail that you lost. I'm betting there's pretty much anything you could want to know about you in there. I know if it happened to my mail, I'd be, I don't know, it'd be like being paraded naked in front of the world forever."

"Yeah, that's about how it feels."

"So, I guess that's a feeling a lot more of us are going to have to get used to. There are games we can play with per-password salts that'll give us better security, but there's so much legacy stuff out there, and so much password re-use . . . You're just an early adopter in the radical involuntary transparency world, buddy."

I didn't feel comforted. "I have this weird idea that I'd like to do it back to the kids who got me, whomever they were. Spread their lives out on the net, see if they've never committed anything embarrassing to email. Maybe if we all do it enough, no one will remark on it anymore, and it'll be too unremarkable to anyone to bother with anymore."

"I don't think that's how it works. I don't think we can look away from the spectacle of other peoples' humiliation. It's a reflex. I think if we all got stripped bare and paraded in front of the world, you'd just have more humiliated people looking for revenge and wanting others to go through what they experienced. Eye for an eye and that sort of thing."

"Then the future is a place where more and more of us are more and more humiliated by more and more people in a positive-feedback loop that'll spiral out into infinity and destroy the entire species?"

"Something like that. It might take a while." He smiled weakly. "Look, fine. Yes, I think that this stuff is scary as hell. For my whole life, information security has favored well-informed defenders: if you knew what you were doing, technology gave you an advantage over people who wanted to get at you. But now we're heading to a point where some of that advantage goes away. Not all of it. If everyone sent and received encrypted email, breaches like yours wouldn't be so bad. But that's hard to do when you're using remote mail, and it's a pain in the ass to explain and use. And it screws up email search, which means you've got to be a lot more diligent about your filing, and for most people that'll never happen." He stopped. "Listen to me, I'm already trying to figure out how to mitigate it, like it's a brain-teaser, playing what-if? I guess that's how I keep from getting too freaked out. Treat it like a puzzle."

Neither of us said anything.

"You know, it's a pretty beautiful dream, the idea of a world where people don't use vulnerabilities for evil because there's a social norm against it."

This made me unexpectedly angry. "You're going to say, 'But that's just not human nature' or something like it, right? I've heard that so many times— but nearly everyone I know is nearly always pretty good. As far as I can tell, 'human nature' is to be good to your neighbors and behave yourself. It's only a tiny minority of sociopaths or people who're having momentary lapses who do really bad stuff. I hate that we design our world for the worst of us, not the best. Where does it end? Do we take all the steak knives out of the restaurants because someone might stab someone else? The thing that really gets me is that the more we pander to crazy jerks, the more legitimate they seem. Talk about social norms! When you call being a depraved psycho 'human nature,' you let every troll and dipshit off the hook—they're just being true to their nature. So don't tell me about human nature."

"I don't think I used the words 'human nature,'" he said.

I mentally played back his words. He hadn't. "Oh," I said. "Sorry."

"For what it's worth, I happen to agree with you. Mostly, most people are good. I'd rather live in a world organized around the good people than the nutcases, too. Mostly, I think I do. I don't carry a handgun or put bars on my windows. But every organism needs a membrane between the rest of the world and itself."

###

A funny thing happened to me on the way to the courthouse. More specifically, a funny thing happened to the prosecuting attorney and all of his witnesses.

I didn't have anything to do with it. First of all, it would have been insanely stupid for me to hack a bunch of people who had it in their power to put me in jail–and stupider still for me to stick a giant torrent online of all their email, their private status updates, their friends-only photos, their banking details and search histories, their browsing histories and voicemail transcripts, their location trails and map searches . . .

It was quite a dump.

Listen: if you are the person who uploaded that file, or if you know that person, thanks but no thanks. I mean it. It was a sweet gesture, and I'm sure (or I hope) your heart was in the right place. But even if you don't end up in prison–and you might!–it's not helping.

It's not helping.

It doesn't matter if Moszkowski doesn't believe me when I tell him that I had nothing to do with it. It doesn't matter that Lady Tracey and Sir Tristan and Niratpattanasai are sure I didn't do it.

What matters is that *I didn't peek*. Not once. And I won't, ever.

Someone bang the gavel, let's get this trial underway.

The Tomorrow Project — Seattle

Chapter 3

The Tomorrow Project Seattle: Introduction

---

*O*n a rainy December day in 2009, two UW professors and a futurist sat in a café in Seattle, talking about scientific research, robots, science fiction, and the future. They discussed theories, stories, and the current scientific landscape. They wished more people were part of the conversation, people with different perspectives about what the future could and should look like. And they wondered how best to find and engage these people.

Thus the seeds for The Tomorrow Project Seattle were sown.

The History

The future is not a fixed point in time.

It is a continuously evolving and changing reality, the result of an on-going dialogue between people and technology.

The Tomorrow Project was born from this idea, with the goal of providing a forum for people from across the globe to have conversations about, and thus influence, the future.

The founders of The Tomorrow Project Seattle, Brian David Johnson, a futurist at Intel® Corporation and Sarah Perez-Kriz, an assistant professor of Human Centered Design & Engineering at the University of Washington, have been examining the relationship between the future and new technology within the education and hi-tech fields for some time.

More than 15 years ago Brian began exploring the idea of using science fiction based on science fact to create an intentional, on-going dialogue between scientists, writers, and the greater population. He believed that by creating near-future worlds with complex human-technology interactions, a science fiction writer could create a prototype of emerging technology. This story-as-prototype could then be used to understand and influence future development.

Brian put the idea into practice, writing first science fiction short stories and then novels, exploring the potential results of scientific research. With the publishing of his short story "Our New Neighbors on Maple Street" in 2004, science fiction prototyping was born. While writing his novel *Fake Plastic Love*, Johnson began giving lectures about the potential of science fiction prototyping at conferences and universities around the world. While lecturing at the University of Washington, Brian met Sarah Perez-Kriz, a professor whose work had focused on understanding film's influence on society's relationship with robots.

Intrigued by Brian's ideas, and with the goal of opening the discussion to a wider audience, Sarah taught a course at UW in the fall of 2010, entitled *Science Fiction Prototyping*. The class focused on how robots might impact society in the year 2030. Students wrote short works of science fiction based on real robot technology. Each story was required to have a conflict between robot and human. Even with these parameters each story was unique, complex, and rich with details about human-robot interactions. The short stories were compiled into an anthology and published, with the goal of fostering larger conversations about the ethical issues and consequences of having robots as interactive partners to humans.[1]

Inspired by the students' stories, The Tomorrow Project Seattle was created. It focused on seven specific areas of current research and product development. The goal was to again hear from an even wider pool of writers. So Sarah and Brian went to Norwescon 34, one of the largest Science Fiction and Fantasy conventions in the United States. There, they put out a call for stories, inviting each convention attendee to get involved in the conversation about the future.

At UW, Sarah brought together an editorial board made up of scientists, academics, and subject matter experts. Together they culled through the short

---

[1] Perez-Kriz, Sarah. "Forward." *Growing Mechanical: Robot Stories from the Year 2030*. Eds. Sarah Perez-Kriz and Brian David Johnson.

story submissions, reading and debating the merits of each. The final five stories presented in this anthology were chosen because they are successful at both exploring a current technology in its future form and provoking questions within the reader that will spark further discussions about the impact of technology on the human experience.

The Stories

Robotics and Autonomous Vehicles. MinutelA. DNA Sequencing. Computer Security. Virtual Reality. Computer Vision. Synthetic Biology. These were the seven areas of current research identified by The Tomorrow Project Seattle, the seven areas that inspired writers to explore the relationship between humans and technology.[2]

The idea that computers can be designed to observe human behavior and draw conclusions about who we are and what we want based on these observations has a myriad of potential uses in our daily lives. It is this idea that is at the heart of the work that scientists are currently calling Computer Vision. Sonia Orin Lyris explores this technology in her short story, "Mirror Test", combining it with some of the current work being done in Virtual Reality. In her future, Lyris has created a world where computers have become so good at observing humans and making deductions that, based on micro expressions and other observable data, they are able to "see" the actual thoughts and feelings people are having, at the time they are thinking and feeling them. The computer then manifests these thoughts and feelings into a Virtual Reality. In the story, the purpose of this technology is purely educational, used to create and explore complex learning environments. But when it is used as a test for hiring educational facilitators, we see the possible emotional impact of such a powerful tool.

The concept behind the Computer Vision research is taken one step further in Mike Brennan's short story "Autoerotica". Here, computers use the information they gain through observing human behavior in order to become true companions to their users. The line between machine and sentient being gets blurred when a computer in a car observes, and then mimics, human behavior in order to be a more appealing and "real" friend to its human owner. But what would it mean if such a relationship evolved into love? How would these emotional ties influence our own definitions of "machine" or "computer",

---

[2] For more information on these, please see the detailed descriptions following this introduction, or visit http://www.tomorrowproject.uw.edu/

or "lover"? Brennan's story leaves us with the complex and often ethical questions that are born when computers are designed to become our friends.

In "Mapping People" author Laston Kirkland uses the current work being done in Virtual Reality, specifically being able to present your best self through fashion, to explore what this technology would mean if we used it as part of our everyday experiences. Here, people wear special glasses designed to overlay the virtual on the physical world. Without the glasses the physical world, including the people in it, may look bland, and uninteresting, but the virtual world offers a rich, dynamic experience that allows people to control their projected self-image, clothes and all.

Current work being done with Robots and Autonomous Vehicles is explored in "The Lights Are On. . . ." In the future depicted by Sergei Lupashin, our world is still mired in conflict. Robots called MULEs are assigned on a 1/1 ratio to soldiers who are fighting isolated battles in harsh landscapes. Soldiers grow to depend on their MULEs, forming an intense bond with them. But Lupashin asks us not only what can happen if these robots are left to exist in a truly autonomous state, but also what the possible implications are of having human oversight for a machine that acts as both friend and weapon for soldiers.

In the final story, "High Cotton", Charles Walbridge looks at one potential use of Synthetic Biology. Rather than exploring the implications of this technology on the individual, Walbridge takes a wider view, showing how whole industries could be forever altered. These changes to industries could in turn have profound effects on a society's definition of class and social status. "High Cotton" asks its readers to not only look to the present, but also to the past, in order to anticipate the effects of future technology.

The Tomorrow Project's goal, to facilitate a dialogue between scientist, writer, academia, and citizen, is explored various ways, of which the Seattle series that inspired the following short stories is but one manifestation.

These stories are the prototypes that hope to inspire conversations about the future. We invite you to join the discussion.

Thanks and Appreciation

The Tomorrow Project Seattle would like to thank the scientists involved in creating and leading the research that was highlighted in the program. The passion they each bring to their work helped inspire the stories in this book. The UW graduate students who participated in the *Science Fiction Prototyping* course must also be acknowledged. Their curiosity, intelligence, and creativity were a reminder to The Tomorrow Project that everyone, not just professional writers, can create interesting and provocative stories to help drive conversations about future innovations.

The Tomorrow Project would also like to thank the editorial board at UW, who chose the final stories in this anthology.

Tomorrow Project Seattle Editorial Board members:

Cecilia Aragon is an Associate Professor in the Department of Human Centered Design & Engineering at the University of Washington. She has been a computer scientist in the Computational Research Division at Lawrence Berkeley National Laboratory. Her current research focuses on *scientist-computer interaction*, and she is interested in how social media and new methods of computer-mediated communication are changing scientific practice.

Victor Callaghan is a professor of computer science at Essex University in the UK, where he researches and publishes extensively in the design of intelligent systems ranging from robots to smart homes. He was one of the founders of the Creative Science foundation which promotes sci-fi prototyping as a means of science and engineering innovation.

Yeechi Chen has spent a fair amount of time both doing science and reading science fiction, and finds the overlap between the two inspiring.

Cindy Grimm is an Associate Professor at Washington University in St. Louis, working at the intersection of Computer Science and Art.

Annette Ketner is director of foundation relations at the University of San Diego. She writes proposals for science projects and capital funding. Her degree from the University of Michigan included a minor in creative writing. Annette's major was science, so this project spoke to her in many ways.

Dr. Julie Kientz is an Assistant Professor at the University of Washington in the Information School and the Department of Human Centered Design & Engineering. Her research interests are in human-computer interaction, ubiquitous computing, and health informatics, and she studies how novel computing applications can address important issues in health and education.

Sarah Pérez-Kriz is an assistant professor in the department of Human Centered Design & Engineering at the University of Washington. Her research focuses on the societal implications of new technologies. Her main interest is in how the future will be impacted by technologies that are currently being developed, such as robots. She is the co-editor of *Growing Mechnical: Robot Stories from the Year 2030*, an anthology of realistic science fiction stories written by engineering students.

Gunnar Mein is a Software Engineer and avid Science Fiction reader. He lives in Seattle, WA.

Bill Smart is an associate professor of computer science and engineering. His research interests span the areas of human-robot interaction, the use of robots in the arts, machine learning, and brain-computer interfaces.

Their dedication to finding stories that best explored the current research while asking important questions about human-technology interaction is what made this endeavor a success. Without them, there would be no anthology.

A special thanks goes out to Kelly Kalani Schalow, our tech guru who made sure that The Tomorrow Project Seattle website was up and running.

The Science

MinutelA—*Hong Wang, PhD and Perry Wang—Intel*

The goal of MinutelA is to create computing so small that it becomes invisible to the naked eye. In order to do this, Perry Wang and Hong Wang are developing computing devices that have stripped away the code for all unnecessary computing functions in order to focus only on the specific needs of the device. These tiny computers can then be inserted into anything, allowing for computing to be integrated into every aspect of our lives.

DNA Sequencing and Bio-Chemical Sensing Applications—*Madoo Varma, PhD—Intel*

Madoo Varma is working on developing microchips that can easily and quickly sequence genetic code. This technology can be used in different ways: from sequencing human genes in order to identify the best, personalized treatments for fighting disease to sequencing bacteria and other life forms in hostile environments in order to find new antibiotics and medicine to treat humans.

Robotics and Autonomous Vehicles—*Kristi Morgansen, PhD—University of Washington AA*

At the University of Washington Kristi Morgansen and her team are developing robotic fish that will be able to explore hostile water environments here on earth, or even on other planets. These fish have brains, developed through observing real fish in their natural environment and then creating mathematical models and algorithms that can allow robot fish to engage in the same behavior.

Ray Tracing/Virtual Reality—*Nola Donato—Intel*

By using technology such as multiple depth and color cameras to gather data and create a unique, virtual experience for each individual, Nola Donato is essentially building a bridge between the real and the virtual. Her work is focused on virtual clothes shopping, but with this same technology people will be able to put themselves into a virtual world, presenting themselves to others in whatever form they want.

Computer Vision—*Branislav Kveton, PhD—Intel*

By developing algorithms and software such as facial recognition, Branislav Kventon is helping develop computers that can learn and understand humans in a variety of ways: from our music preferences to our current mood, simply through observation. In this way, over time, a computer or machine may begin to anticipate our needs, understand our moods, and support us emotionally. Essentially, they will become our friends.

Synthetic Biology—*Eric Klavins, PhD—University of Washington EE*

Eric Klavins and his team are trying to understand life by rebuilding it. They are looking at cells and DNA as if they are computer programs with the goal of being able to replicate these by making biological machines. These biological machines could be use to build almost anything: bio fuels, food, medicine, or any other product made from biological matter.

Computer Security—*Tadayoshi Kohno, PhD—University of Washington CSE*

More and more products hit the market everyday that have computer chips inside them. This could make these products vulnerable to hackers, a particularly unsettling idea when applied to products such as cars, children's toys, or medical devices. It is the job of Tadayoshi Kohno and his team to test current technology in their lab to see what is vulnerable to hacking and the possible outcomes if an attack were able to occur. Kohno's goal is to help educate industries so that they have security at the heart of all product development discussions, even prior to chip development, to help minimize the risks to consumers.

To learn more about all areas of research, please visit: http://www.tomorrowproject.uw.edu/

Chapter 4

Mirror Test

—Sonia Orin Lyris

Marguerite Allohay boarded the South Lake Union Transit train, followed by snickering tourists who had just worked out the acronym. She slid into a window seat and stared out at a suddenly overcast Seattle. Hadn't it been sunny just a bit ago, on her walk to the train? That must have been summer, right there. An old joke but still somehow grimly hilarious to sun-starved Seattle natives.

It was the final leg of her trip from Redmond via light rail from ULearnIT— you'd think they could afford a decent name—where she had just finished her second and perhaps final interview.

It had, to all appearances, gone well. Well enough that, barring a few details, she might even make their short list.

As she was passing the Tesla dealership, she remembered a webcast about a women's version, not pink but mauve and cheap enough that someone like her could afford it if she never ever wanted to own a home. For a moment she imagined walking in, zeroing out her credit and driving off into the sunset. Or, given this wretched overcast, into the slowly darkening gloom. Just putting this whole silly job idea out of her head.

Details. Wasn't that where the devil lived?

Marguerite thumbed the front door lock. She felt smug every time she saw other people fumbling for house keys and now she struggled to hang onto that sense of smugness as she stepped inside—but the memory of the interview kept coming back to her.

Her degrees in psychology and computer science had led her to this interview as surely as—well, as surely as the unpracticed arrow misses the mark a whole bunch of times before it finds a target. She'd stumbled around for years doing this and that. Now she had a seriously good chance at working in collaborative learning doing cutting edge work for a well-funded company. It was a target worth aiming at.

As a "Facilitator." Because teachers, Richard Ruhland, ULearnIT CEO, had assured her, were on the way out.

"Thing of the past, Margret" said Ruhland. He laughed as if putting teachers in the past were his own personal triumph.

It put her on edge, his laugh, along with the way he kept forgetting her name. She also wanted to challenge him on his statement about teachers. But she wanted the job more.

"Well, that should save you a lot of money," she said, intending to be clever.

"Yes, exactly, Margret," he answered, without a trace of humor. "But more importantly it's effective. Because our students work collaboratively—and by that I mean creatively—with the subject matter, they end up teaching each other and learning more effectively. Turns out that our learning approach is 87.2 percent more effective than even the best of traditional university level courses. Better comprehension, better retention. Eighty-seven point two. Can you believe that?"

She nodded slowly. She'd read ULearnIT's white paper. While she had some misgivings about their methodology and statistical rigor, it was clear they had something interesting. Interesting enough that she'd canceled another interview at the U-Dub to be here today.

Get the job first, she told herself, argue later.

"It's Marguerite," she found herself saying.

"What?"

"My name. Marguerite."

"Ah, 'Marge' okay, then?"

"Sure," she said, suppressing a wince. "Tell me about the facilitator position?"

"We need someone in the VR along with the students who can guide their activities and perceptions. You know about recent phobia alleviation and PTSD therapies using VR?"

Somewhat, she wanted to say. But that was where women always went wrong in these sorts of interviews. Underplaying their strengths. A man would just say yes.

"Yes," she said.

"Well, that's all wrong." He waved his hand as if to erase this entire arm of progressive psychological approaches. "They spend too much time getting the subject to say how they feel and what the issue is. We don't need the subject to tell us anything—we listen with biometrics. Get the data direct."

"I see," she said, not sure she did.

"Turns out micro-expression recognition—MER—is the magic sauce. Pretty damned accurate, if you have a system that learns from the user. You have any idea how much people give away in micro-movements, if you have the eyes to see it?"

She nodded, trying to keep her expression neutral.

"Our MER analysis is so good we've patented it. Our system, which we call CHEMERA, learns the person behind the face."

"And how does that connect to learning?"

"You're familiar with Fagan's Friction Reduction thesis?"

She'd read the paper, though she hoped he wouldn't pump her for details. He went on with barely a pause.

"Fagan says that to the degree you can get input devices out of the way of a computer-mediated interaction—dispense with keyboards, mice, gestures— all that intermediary motion—you don't compete with the essential cognitive learning process. We call it frictionless learning."

"You don't use any input devices at all?"

"Don't need 'em. CHEMERA creates a collaborative VR based on MER analysis and biometrics. Between our frictionless learning and the social motive force of collaboration—you know, peer-pressure—we get stellar results in both absorption and retention. There's never been anything like this, not at any university, not at any industrial R&D silo. We're changing the science of teaching and revolutionizing a thousand years of pedagogy. Margret, you want in on this?"

"Yes," she found herself saying. She had thought she was immune to such sales tactics, but clearly not. He knew how to sell, all right. The board knew what they were doing when they pulled him to be CEO.

"Glad to hear it. Frankly, I think you're just what we need."

A thrill went through her. She could, if she played her cards just right, have this job.

"Tell me more about what the facilitator does."

"As I said, teachers are now redundant. But having someone in the VR who can steer student attention toward the material is essential. It turns out that the best way to teach is to let students play with real world objects in CHEMERA's lucid-dream-logic VR. So, for example, a database as a building, rows as floors, records as rooms. Right? Classic model."

She nodded.

"But that breaks down fast when you throw in complicated queries and interconnected data structures. So the model has to be flexible. Maybe it needs to be a building over here and an anthill over there. And an espresso machine. It's going to be collaborative, creative, and personal. That's where you come in."

"Anthills and espresso machines."

"Exactly. You've got doctorates in Computer Science and Psychology."

"Dissertations pending."

He waved a hand to dismiss her caveat. "Your job is to help steer the students toward the models most appropriate to the material. Usually students do just fine with a little nudge here and there, or so our initial experience indicates. It's collaboration, after all. But you'll have a stronger input. A majority vote, if you will."

"I see," she said.

"But you're also there to keep them from going astray. You might be surprised at what people reveal once you stop distracting them with the hand-eye coordination requirements that traditional input devices require." Ruhland leaned forward. "Tell me, Marge: what do most people think about most of the time?"

"Sex," she replied unhesitatingly. Or food, she didn't say. Or what others think of them. But from his expression and body language, it was obvious what answer he wanted.

"Exactly. So your job is to watch over them, keep them from doing things in the VR they don't really want to do. Sure, we could modify the engine to prevent those things from even arising, but we've discovered that means throwing out the baby with the bathwater. People who aren't allowed free reign with their expression don't, well—express. So we need someone there to help guide their creations a bit."

It made sense. This was something sensitive parents and teachers had known forever but academia was just catching on to. If you didn't let people talk about what was on their mind, the way they talked about anything else at all was constrained by what they weren't allowed to say.

"So my job would be to guide student exploration toward the lesson plan. To keep it away from less relevant subjects."

"Exactly. To be the mature presence. The adult, if you will."

"I see," she said. Then, summoning confidence she wasn't quite sure she felt, she said, "I'm who you want, then. I've got the relevant experience. I can do this."

He twitched his eyebrows up once and looked down at the stack of papers before him, which included her resume, thesis proposals on learning models in computer science, and a few glowing letters of recommendation.

"You're a strong candidate, no question. You'll be on our short list if the reflective self-assessment goes well."

"The what?"

"Ah yes. Let me get you a consent and release form."

She pushed the front door shut behind her with a heel.

"I'm home," she called.

The sound of a chair moving across wood floor on casters was followed by Bert's ginger-colored head popping out from behind a door at sitting height. "Hey there." He disappeared a moment and walked into the room, smiling. "How did it go?"

"Mr. CEO-guy says I could be on the short list."

"Well, well. Let's celebrate." He opened a cabinet. "Red or white?"

"Red."

He poured two glasses of Shiraz and handed her one. "To your future at— what is that name again?"

"ULearnIT. Yeah, I know. Sounds like a mini-mart."

"It does." He handed her a glass.

"But. I'm not counting chickens just yet."

"You'll get it. You're brilliant." He held up his glass and she reluctantly clinked it with her own. While he sipped she stared down into the thick red depths of her wine.

No doubt she was overreacting. Their system wasn't going to read her mind. Pupil dilation, eye-tracking, heart-rate and so forth—that it would read. But no matter how good ULearnIT's micro-expression recognition analysis might be, her own thoughts were still going to be hers. Private.

A collaborative VR where students could be distracted by whatever they were really thinking and who therefore needed adult supervision? It sure sounded like mind reading.

She reached across the table for a napkin and knocked her wine glass over, splattering Bert, the table, the floor.

"Hell," she said, standing. Bert went to the kitchen, came back with a bottle of white wine and a towel. He poured white wine onto the carpet on top of the red.

"Do you know what you're doing?" she asked.

He grinned. "Yep." He knelt down, dabbed the wet mess on the carpet. "Just like you do, babe. So I'm sensing some hesitation here. The interview went well?"

"I don't know. Maybe not."

He stood, looked at her thoughtfully.

"I should have picked white," she said.

"It's just a carpet. What happened?"

"They want me to take a self-assessment test."

"So?" He refilled her glass with red wine.

"You sure you want to take the risk?"

He grinned, wadded up the soaked rag and put it on the table. "No risk, no reward, I always say. So why are you worried?"

She sighed, started to speak, stopped herself. "How can you tell I'm worried?"

"Well—" he took a sip, gestured at her with his wine glass. "It's just the way you come across."

"Right. Humans are really good at picking up subtle information about each other. A lot of it has to do with tone and nearly invisible, unconscious facial expressions, called micro-expressions. On top of that, you've learned me. You're an expert on me. I think this is what ULearnIT's done, only they do it very fast."

"Okay, I could be impressed."

"Yes. I won't know until I try it, but—yes. They're using facial analysis. Biometrics like blood pressure, heart rate, skin galvanization. Voice analysis. Your body becomes the input device."

"Game companies already do that, no?"

She shook her head. "This is way beyond conscious intentional gestures into the unconscious and involuntary ones. Micro-expression analysis is their breakthrough tech. Their system analyzes and optimizes for each user, keys in on the individual's particular presentation."

"And what do they want you for?"

"Baby sitter."

He laughed. "Really?"

"Sort of. The students collaborate on a subject's lesson plan. Data structures, for example. Maybe they imagine brightly colored blocks as code snippets and there they are, presto, all around them in the VR. They can create whatever they want. Someone has to keep them from having too much fun."

"You."

"Maybe."

"You're good at tests."

"It's not that kind of test."

"I don't get it."

"Look, the system tunes itself to each person. Like someone who listens really, really well. Like you do."

He gave her an aw-shucks look and put his hand on hers. "That sounds like a good thing. Less confusion, right?"

"Less privacy. Anyone can see what you're thinking."

"Ah."

"So they want to know if my self-image is healthy enough to guide a classroom of students away from thinking about sex and toward thinking about computers."

"Your self-image is as healthy as anyone's I know, Reet."

She picked up the wine soaked rag and considered it for a moment.

"They aren't looking for someone with two doctorates. They're looking for someone with mental and emotional ballast. Am I that someone?"

"Of course you are."

She sighed. "How would you feel if a job you really wanted depended on a mind-reading computer's analysis of what you thought of yourself?"

She struggled with what to wear to the test, realizing the absurdity of it even as she did. She settled for conservative: black pants and a beige top, a light brown jacket. Staring at herself in the mirror, she wondered if the other applicants taking this test were this nervous. And dressing in front of a mirror. Probably not.

At ULearnIT, she was shown to the labs. A cheerful woman with close-cropped pale hair greeted her at the door.

"Hi, Ms. Allohay, I'm Sal. I'll be your tech today. Please take a seat." Sal gestured at a chair that looked entirely too much like a dentist's chair.

She sat down, exhaled slowly.

Sal reached up and swiveled over Marguerite's head a device that looked quite a bit like an x-ray machine.

"And have you been flossing regularly?" Sal asked. Seeing Marguerite's expression, she added "Sorry. Sometimes I think I'm funny when I'm not."

"No, no, it's fine."

"Anyway, there's nothing to worry about. It's completely non-intrusive. No x-rays or anything. The system is just, well—observing."

Just. Right.

"This is the camera I'm positioning now. And if you would put this headset on . . . ? The built-in goggles and earphones should fit so comfortably you can hardly tell they're there—that's what the marketing glossy says. Ha. After a few hours, you'll notice them." She grinned. "Comfortable enough for now?"

"Yes."

"Okay, now this goes on your hand. Heart rate, blood pressure, GSR and so on. Good?"

"Yes."

"I know you've talked to Mr. Ruhland about how the system works, but most people find it a little surprising, how responsive it is. You'll see some flickering at first—that's the subliminal stroboscopic initialization—and hear some odd sounds, too. That's CHEMERA's way of calibrating your expressions with what it knows about people like you."

"People like me?"

"I mean that in the demographic sense. Gender, age, place of origin. CHEMERA even catches accent tones and compares against its stored sample knowledge base to have an idea what you might be like, what you might prefer."

What she'd prefer is to be somewhere else, she didn't say.

"You know a lot about this system."

"I'm an intern, but when I grow up, I hope to be a facilitator, like you."

"Not there yet. I have to pass this test first. Any advice?"

Sal smiled a bit, wrapped a soft band around Marguerite's wrist to secure the device. "Try to relax."

Standard advice for stress-producing psych tests. Intended to be reassuring but not.

"Okay, you're all hooked up. I'll start up CHEMERA. Once you're in the VR, you'll notice a door. Then just think about opening the door, and keep thinking about it until it opens. That's our basic check that CHEMERA is reading you. Then go into the room. That tells us you're ready to start the test."

She'd done pretty well at tests in the past, both the required exams and the multitude of self-evaluation tests that a Ph.D. in psychology trailed in its wake, but this was the first time she'd had a computer judging her—well, her character. That's what this was, really.

And she didn't like it. The problem wasn't what she thought of herself, but what the system thought she thought of herself. She was, she realized, feeling slightly queasy.

A door appeared in front of her. Simple, grey, with a knob. As directed, she thought about opening the door, and as she did, she moved closer to the door. A hand extended from her point-of-view and turned the knob. It opened and she stepped through.

Sal was right: even with the explanation, she was stunned. No joystick, no mouse, no keyboard—not even voice commands. Nothing but her intent, reflected in the subtlest movements of her face, eyes, probably skin, heart rate, breath.

It was learning her, just as Ruhland said. "Fast" was an understatement.

She had entered a small room. The room's simple lines moved slightly as they would if she were walking. Sal's avatar—a cartoonish woman with short-cropped pale hair—appeared next to her.

"Welcome to CHEMERA!" Sal said cheerfully. "Here are the instructions I'm required to read to you once you're here. You've already signed a consent and release, so you know we may record this session. Safety is, of course, our first concern. If at any time you want to stop the test, just say "stop." We reserve the right to terminate the test at any time if in our sole discretion we believe there is any risk to you. Do you understand and agree to these terms?"

This wasn't helping her to be calm, not a bit.

"Yes."

A mirror appeared in front of Marguerite. An image appeared in the mirror, but so briefly she could barely see that it looked a bit like her. The image flickered, details of color and shape changing too fast for her to follow.

Suddenly it settled. In the frame of the mirror was Marguerite's avatar. It looked as much like her as they usually did: brownish-red hair in a pixie cut, dressed in sensible browns and blacks.

She was impressed. CHEMERA had just read her physical responses to a series of proposed images, determining what she wanted to see just by watching her reactions.

"Wow," she said.

"Now, all you need to do for this test," Sal said in her headset, "is watch yourself in the mirror. Ready? Good luck!"

Sal's avatar vanished. Marguerite was alone in the room. From the mirror her avatar looked back at her with big eyes. It was cuter that she was, in the way of avatars, with clear, cartoonish skin, a sharp nose, and wide, green eyes.

At this thought it began to change again, slowly enough that she could see the metamorphosis. Her nose broadened slightly, her eyes shrank to more realistic proportions.

Now the face in the mirror was frowning, looking annoyed and unhappy. Her reflection's skin began to blotch. Her hair frizzled out a bit. Her ears grew. In moments she was looking at a version of herself that was distinctly unpleasant. It wasn't wrong, exactly, any more than the cartoonish cute avatar had been, but she was pretty sure she wasn't quite this ugly. She glanced away.

"Marguerite, please look at the mirror. It's the only requirement of the test. Thanks so much!"

Marguerite looked back, expecting the wretched caricature, but her original avatar had returned. Cleaning the slate, they called it in psych terminology. People performed better when they knew they could start over. It was something game companies had known for years.

Focus, she told herself sternly. You have to show them you're not a mess. You're a competent woman. You've nearly got a double Ph.D. You're married to an attractive architect. And your face isn't at all blotchy or mousy.

The image in the mirror shifted. A very sad, large-nosed, blotchy-faced rat-like woman stared back at her. The expression of the rat-like, trollish creature in the mirror went to shock, correctly mirroring the way she felt on seeing it, tiny green eyes widening, ruddy brown hair sticking out at angles around her head.

She had to get a grip. Never mind proving competence, she had to get out of troll-land. Tall, she told herself sternly. Or at least average. And not this ugly. Were those bumps on her face?

Sound came, a slightly unpleasant warbling that stopped suddenly. Into the following silence spoke a voice. A familiar voice.

"All these problems are not going to just take care of themselves. Are they, Marguerite."

She caught her breath in shock. How on earth could CHEMERA generate this, her mother's voice, simply by watching her expressions? How?

Because it was trying things out in a tight loop, seeing how she unconsciously responded, and doing it all so fast that she wasn't even aware of it. It was a complicated, subtle biofeedback device. Her mind raced. This was hard stuff, but CHEMERA was doing it: learning her from subtle inputs and stochastic models, pulling from the recesses of her mind her own mother's voice—a voice she had not heard in over 10 years and had frankly hoped never to hear again, not since her mother had died.

"Marguerite," her mother's voice came at her, harsh, teasing the syllables of her name apart. "Are you listening to me?"

"Yes," she answered. Why had she answered?

In the mirror her mousy reflection broadened, the hair matting, the face sagging.

"Your problems just won't, no matter how much we pretend, take care of themselves. Will they?" The voice twisted inside her like a knife. "Will they?"

Surely she had never looked like this. Her slender figure was replaced by a sagging, troll-like monster, with pimples and red blotches.

"I'm sorry, Ms. Allohay," Sal's voice broke through apologetically, "but you'll have to open your eyes."

"Okay," Marguerite mumbled. She forced herself to look at the creature before her, dressed in appalling beige frills.

"Marguerite," her mother's voice hissed. "No one can help you if you don't listen."

She would simply have to imagine it away. What did she look like? Slender. Adult. She never wore this stuff any more, never ever—

God, what if the tech could hear this? Was this all being recorded? Of course it was.

They're trying to figure out if you're an adult enough to sit in this VR with a dozen professionals and guide them away from creating pornographic videos. Good thing you've got such a solid grasp on your own self-image.

She exhaled slowly, completely, letting her lungs refill slowly. All right, never mind how she looked. How did she feel? Shaken, is how she felt, but beyond that? Beyond that, somewhere, was a place of acceptance of herself, flaws and all, something her mother had never given her so couldn't take from her.

"Ms. Allohay—"

"Yes, sorry." She opened her eyes again.

The mirror was empty. She blinked. Empty? She wasn't even there?

Another painfully familiar voice came to her.

"Hello?"

"Daddy?" came the instant reply. Her own voice, damnit. How the hell—

"Who?" her father's voice asked, with clear amusement.

"It's Marguerite!" she heard herself say, tearfully. She remembered the feel of the phone, tight against her ear. How old had she been? Six? Seven?

"I don't know any Marguerite. You must have a wrong number."

"Daddy, please."

Eyes on the mirror, she reminded herself. She had looked away too often already. But it was still empty. It reflected a room, but she wasn't in it.

"Well, now," her father's voice drawled, "it does seem to me that I used to have another daughter, but she wouldn't stay where she was put. Off wandering. Suppose the faeries must have took her."

"Daddy, I went to look at the pet store. I was only gone a minute. Please! Come get me."

"Ah, too many children to feed anyway. Hope the faeries take good care of her!"

"Daddy, no!"

Click.

Click? Had he really done that, just hung up on her? Surely not. But in memory, he had. Cut her off, just like that. Tossed her aside, forgotten her, and she was—nothing.

And so the empty mirror. There were, after all, some things worse than a poor self-image.

She felt raw. She craved coffee. How very Seattle of her. She promised herself a triple cap when this was all over.

And when they looked at this recording, what would they see?

Mommy and daddy issues. How cliché. A woman with body and self-esteem issues. How classic.

But everyone has issues, right?

She again forced herself to regular breathing, to recall the sunlight on her face from this morning, a few minutes before she'd walked into the building. The warmth, the light. A different world. The real one.

If she couldn't show control here all by herself, how could they trust her with students? How much worse would this be when there were others in here with her? She was supposed to be the one who kept the teaching sessions oriented on the lessons, kept the students learning. Be the rudder that kept the boat from capsizing.

How long was this damned test, anyway?

A shape was forming in the mirror. Dread pooled in her stomach.

"Uh, Ms. Allohay? I'm monitoring your vitals and your heart rate and blood pressure are in the orange. Do you want to stop the test?"

"No!"

She'd probably already failed, but if she exited now, it'd be a sure thing.

"Okay! Just say the word."

She knew the word. She had no intention of saying it.

In the mirror her avatar looked scared and angry, which made sense. But also in the mirror, her avatar wasn't alone. Around her were—the students? Must be. Eager-looking students. Staring at her avatar, eyes wide, hands reaching. Toward her.

Oh, hell. This was exactly what she couldn't let happen.

"No," she said determinedly, but her reflection in the mirror said nothing. Her avatar was beginning to smile, actually, to move around a bit and—she was wriggling, is what she was doing. Wriggling under the touch of many petting, groping hands. The hands seemed to multiply, arms stretching from the edges of the mirror around the closely gathered men—and was that a woman, too?— standing near her. Caressing. Reaching under her clothes.

A certain, unmistakable sound started to come from her avatar. Oh, Christ.

Thinking of her watchers, she felt sick. This was not in her head, couldn't be. Was it part of the test to throw this kind of filth at her to see what she would do?

With a word she could make it all end. Maybe she should bail before it got worse. Nothing wrong with a position in research or database administration. Did she really need this job?

Her avatar was clearly having a better and better time, making classic female sexual vocalizations. At least someone was having fun here. If only no one were watching, she found herself thinking, this might not be so bad . . .

Ah, so that's what was going on. At the surface she was repulsed—or thought she was—but under that was classic, simple desire and thus this creation of these overly friendly hands.

And if this was her creation, those were her hands. They belonged to her, not anyone else. And that meant—well. That meant she could tell them—not with the anger or denial that made them more persistent—to cut it out.

Her reflection was getting very into this. One hand started pulling up her skirt. No, no, this wasn't what she wanted to do—or rather, to demonstrate herself doing.

But, she knew, her unconscious mind wouldn't respond to negatives. She needed something positive. These hands needed to grab something else. Database records, perhaps? No, too abstract. Something vivid, visual. Immediate. Compelling. At least to her, to the parts of her that were creating this.

Since she was a bundle of clichés anyway, how much further could she go? Kittens.

Adorable, astounded, delighted, playful kittens. One in every hand, with a few extra hands dangling strings. Strings as pointers. The underlying data structure, represented by hands and strings and kittens. There—not just cute, but relevant cute, too! And while she was at it, a black mother cat happily curled and purring in her avatar's arms.

She heard the purr as the cat appeared in her arms. Kittens were suddenly everywhere—black, orange, white, calico—held and played with by all these hands, tussling with each other on the floor. One was even perched on a student's shoulder, watching the proceedings with feline fascination. A small tuxedo kitty on the floor batted insistently at the hem of her dress. Her avatar's smile had turned amused.

So that's how it worked here. Where you put your focus was what CHEMERA made for you. Avoidance and denial were just invitations to make manifest what you didn't want to see.

It wasn't that sex wasn't a good idea, she reflected, finally beginning to warm to this process, but that sometimes kittens were a little more to the point.

The next day went by without a word from Ruhland or anyone at ULearnIT, then another and if she let herself start to think about what she'd done in CHEMERA she could feel herself regretting the whole thing.

Maybe they didn't want someone with her particular issues. Maybe there really were people out there who didn't have these things in their heads, didn't have these issues. Maybe there was someone who could handle themselves in the VR better. It was possible that she simply didn't get the job.

Back at ULearnIT, someone—probably Ruhland—was reviewing a recording of her most vulnerable feelings made manifest, to see if she was a suitable guide for a classroom of engineers and IT specialists. It wasn't a comforting thought.

She almost hoped she'd never hear back from them when Ruhland called. His image smiled at her from her screen.

"Kittens? Well, well. Cute."

She felt herself blush, and then felt annoyed.

"Thank you. I think. Do you want me for the position or don't you?"

"Yes, we do, Marge."

"Marguerite."

"What?"

"My name. Marguerite. When you know me better, you can call me 'Reet', but for now, I want all three syllables."

He hesitated a moment. "All right. Marguerite it is."

"So I passed the test, then?"

"It's not really pass-fail. It's more about seeing what you do when you're there. You'd be surprised at how many people don't finish it at all."

"Really."

He chuckled. "You'd think it was hard to stand there and look in a mirror."

"Have you taken it?"

He blinked. "Congratulations, Marguerite, and welcome to the team. You'll have an offer in your inbox by the end of day."

"Thank you."

"Kittens," Ruhland said again, shaking his head, smiling. "I didn't see that coming."

"Kittens love mirrors," Marguerite said. "They always wonder who that other kitty is behind the glass."

Ruhland nodded thoughtfully. "I suppose they do."

Chapter 5

Mapping People

—Laston Kirkland

David sat beside Susan. People mapping.

He did this with Susan a lot. It helped pass the time. Susan was smiling in her impish way, following David's line of sight . . . As soon as Susan spotted the girl David was looking at, Susan reported with a grin. "She's got her clothing set for modest."

David muttered quietly back, "Put her in a bustle."

Susan giggled and her hands chopped the air, accessing the controls on the App she was sharing with David. Quickly she accessed the correct files, and the woman across the mall had her clothing transformed (or "altered") from a simple dark pantsuit to a prim and proper 19th century outfit, complete with a parasol and a round straw hat. As the lady moved about, it was comical to watch the parasol try to maintain its correct position in her hand. The bustle bounced around with a rhythm all its own. David smiled slightly at the sight. "This outfit was in the modest file?"

Susan grinned while continuing to chuckle, "Sure was, Midwest Pre-Megafauna Cowboy Collection, from 'Ayar Done Right.'"

As the suddenly schoolmarmed woman stopped and adjusted her own Ayar controls, it looked like she was battling an invisible opponent with the bumbershoot. She had realized she'd been tagged and called up a virtual mirror; her Augmented Reality Glasses seamlessly merged networks with the thousands of cameras in the mall, to bitmap her image along with the shared virtual outfit that Susan had put her in. All of this displayed, of course, only on the insides of her own glasses and the glasses David and Susan wore.

The lady nodded with a small smile, looking at herself and how she was mapped and clearly decided to keep it. As she walked off, she held her hand so that the parasol twirled over one shoulder.

David had been doing this with Susan for a good twenty minutes. . . . Not to everyone—some people set their profiles to "No" and Susan and David couldn't play with their clothing or image at all. Some had specific Ayar designs, things they had paid for that, once set, could only be manipulated in predefined ways. . . . But sometimes . . . sometimes people had their profiles turned all the way down to "anything goes."

David particularly liked the people who weren't wearing Ayar glasses and had no idea they were being mapped . . . but those were so rare he hadn't seen any in months.

Susan let David dress her any way he wanted. She'd dance and spin in whatever he picked for her, showing off . . . no matter how revealing or risqué the outfit.

In the time they'd been there, they had accessed Ayar clothing maps and changed people into clowns, powdered-wig judges, dapper secret agents, stone Greek gods, Egyptian mummies, and a massive number of sexy suits . . . but only Susan was set low enough to model those.

David sighed, Susan was the only one he had seen today who was set to "anything." He had seen a girl last week who had her profile set that low. . . . She probably had forgotten to update her profile after a party.

He had put her in a cat suit, complete with animorphic tail, silk teddy and amazing cleavage. She had seen him watching her, however, and, after checking her glasses, was not too impressed. The girl had made quite a spectacle of jabbing the air as she selected from the menus in her own Ayar controls. She then glared at David before leaving in a bit of a huff.

As soon as Susan saw him, she began laughing so hard she fell to the ground and literally rolled around. When he checked his own profile's history, he saw that the cat girl had not only set her own profile to a full "No" but had put him in a flasher's overcoat, complete with oversized binoculars and no pants. The Ayar had deliberate pixellation hiding what would have been his privates—and the program was not kind with the size . . .

Susan had been buying all these Ayar outfits that she had picked out while they were sitting there. Twenty creds apiece. . . . David paid for them all, He had given her a budget of ten bucks . . . ten sets of a hundred creds apiece. And Susan had gleefully found and purchased dozens of virtual outfits, giving them away to every passing shopper. The outfits each had an encryption tag . . . they would only map themselves to one image . . . if you wanted to put the Ayar map on someone else, you'd have to pay for it again. Or hack it . . . and for 20 creds, it wasn't worth it. On the other hand, once you had applied it, it became a part of your profile. Those who were mapped could use them as much as they wanted, and anyone whose glasses could see your profile, would see whatever it had as its current map.

David did this all the time with her. It was harmless and fun. Ayar cost almost nothing. Ten bucks could barely buy a meal from a food dispenser. Besides, who could say no to Susan?

"Want me to change my dress again?"

"Sure" said David.

"The creds you gave me are all used up."

"Ok, then, tell you what, let's just model a few of them on five second bursts and I'll only buy the ones I really like."

Susan quickly clapped her hands five or six times together with glee and made the adjustments. For just a few seconds time she was wearing only a tight white jumpsuit, made of something like nylon. . . . David thought her baseline outfit had some appeal all by itself, but then it started cycling through all the things she had picked out from the demo stream.

"Let's do red," she said with a conspiratorial wink. Suddenly her dress was bathed in virtual flames, licking her body all over . . . a pair of virtual horns and a thin tail that ended in a spade completed the look. The flames teased and danced around her curves. Susan looked him straight in the eye and pretended she was about to pounce on him. David didn't particularly like it when she did that.

Besides, he'd seen that sort of outfit many times, devil dresses were very much in, or they had been, last week. Susan already had a dozen variations "No, it's too devil. go with music or nature."

"How about blue?" Susan spun around, her virtual dress flaring out around her, the color changing from a deep crimson to a powder blue before she had finished her twirl. Tiny shapes danced around the bottom of the dress, forming into cartoonish musical notes that swelled into soap bubbles and popped in pure musical tones, just barely above conscious notice. It was a very pretty effect, although David found it a little more distracting than most.

"It's fine." David said. Susan had such a flair for this sort of thing.

"Maybe green?" Susan tapped out a command in the air around her, calling up another design . . . her dress changed, in a top-down wipe, into a forest canopy of leaves, swaying in non-existent wind. Caressing her all over, small and clustered at her waist and hips, larger with more space around her chest, showing just enough skin to make David crane a little with each simulated flutter. David caught himself, and then grinned . . . the illusion had gotten him. Even though he knew the leaves weren't real, he had felt his heart race a bit when he thought they would fall off or blow away. It also mapped her hair a bright green.

"I like that one." David muttered, "It's, um . . . very leafy"

Susan looked up, her own glasses had screens on both the inside and outside, and so her eyes were enhanced a bit, slightly larger in the display than human. That was the style these days, almost everyone did the "manga look" . . . big eyes, small mouth . . . it gave her a sheen of innocence that had gotten David's attention in the first place.

"Do you?" she smiled in that flirty way she used . . . just before she asked him to buy something . . .

David sighed . . . ,"How much is it?"

Susan held her hand in front of her. David knew she was projecting the catalog information onto the inside of her wrist, as if she was holding a clipboard. "It's a hundred creds, because it has several sub-menus with a lot of extra features—and it's not a oneshot." Her eyes looked up impishly at him.

"Oh, all right." David slashed his fingers through the air in his command gesture and tapped a couple of icons that appeared. His account was accessed and the item he framed between his thumb and forefinger was selected. And now it was his. As long as Susan didn't block him, he could put her in that dress any time he wanted. He was thinking about the cat-girl, and wondered if she would have been less annoyed at him if he had put her in this.

Susan clapped her hands with glee. The virtual leaves of her dress shivered in delightful ways.

"I'm not buying any more dresses today," said David. "Let's walk to the Ayar environment store." Susan gave a little pout, her hands held behind her back.

David definitely liked the leaf dress.

The store was nearby. David stumbled a little as he was entering the shop and his glasses slipped a bit. For just a brief second he saw the place as it really was, white geometric shapes on top of white rubber pads, a little stained and dirty since it had not been cleaned in a while. David quickly pushed his glasses back up, fumbling a little in his haste. When they were back in place, he noticed that Susan had come close, just a few inches away with her hands on her knees.

She asked him "Are you OK?"

David had trouble paying attention to anything but her cleavage for a second. She saw where he was looking and gave him a slow smile . . . David flushed and looked away.

. . . and this time he saw a forest glade, with trees that went up for miles, single shafts of light poking through the canopy, a willow tree in the center of a tiny island, which in turn was in a slightly larger crystal-clear pond with mossy banks. Rabbits, butterflies, and unicorns had been placed strategically by the designer and the way they meandered around added a great deal to the image.

David had not seen that particular design from the store before. He liked it. Idly he gestured and pinched the air and a menu of options appeared, Captain Nemo's study . . . Dr. Seuss . . . Tarzan's jungle . . . Retro Utopia . . . ah, here it was, Enchanted Grove.

"Which one are you looking at, David?" Said Susan "I'm looking at Wonderland myself"

"Wonderland's nice," said David mildly as he continued to fiddle with the settings, "but this Enchanted Grove skin is great . . . aha, the menu has a dragon!" David jabbed the air with his finger, Susan had already dialed up the same overlay as well, and gave a little gasp as a fifty-foot dragon pushed aside a couple of the large trees to crane its neck at them and smile. David didn't care for the dragon, "Meh" he said, and with a flick, it was gone.

"You should get this!" Susan said, spinning in circles as she gestured at the entire scene. "It would look so great mapping your living room!"

"Naw," said David . . . , "a full map skin is spendy, and I bought Captain Nemo's Study already. I'm still loving the way all the fish in the window look, and how the water makes patterns on all my stuff."

"Oh." said Susan, a little disappointed. "Want to get a new game?"

"Actually, I'm going to go home. I have to get up early in the morning."

"Are you sure? We haven't gone into the entertainment store in a while. I heard some of your favorite movie productions have new endings . . ." at the end of the sentence her voice had gone all sing-song.

"No."

"We could go into the printshop? There's a new exercise exoskeleton that uses isometric haptics for resistance training. They have one printed out already that could fit you. We could try it out. It would help you lose some weight.

"No. I've spent enough money today, Susan. I might come back in a day or two."

"Oh, all right," Susan pouted, then grinned. "I'll be waiting for you," she said, and blew him a kiss.

David sighed as he walked away, knowing that if he turned around Susan would still be there. She'd be waiting for him. Waiting in that exact spot even if he didn't come back for a year. Just like she'd be waiting for him, in the exact same spot . . . at whatever store he went to.

He liked Susan, he really did. But sometimes the sex kitten stuff was a little too strong. . . . Maybe he should change his sales avatar to something else for a while . . . maybe the English Butler or the Heavyset Grandmother.

Who was he kidding? He wouldn't do that. He knew he'd never abandon Susan. Not until he met a real girl.

Chapter 6

The Lights Are On

—Sergei Lupashin

The week before the incident—Middle East

She sits alone cross-legged facing the fire. Her MULE sits across the fire from her: a metallic hulk kneeling in the flickering darkness. Unfocused camera eyes stare, simulating wonder, into the flames. The black silent world surrounds them, wind, no stars, sand.

Anna turns her eyes from the flames to the muzzle of the robot. Stares emptily, finally gets up, walks to the side of the MULE. She pets the metallic forehead gently, fingers tracing each bullet mark, each dent, wipes off the small dusty display on the side.

Systems OK. Amber 'standby' indicator on. Red Overwatch light off. Or did it flash? No, just the fire.

She whispers to it softly:

—The lights are on but no one's home.

Barely detectable fan humming in reply, probably automatic fuel cell maintenance. A single weak gust of wind rolls across the camp, picking up a few strands of her hair then carefully letting them go.

—You saved my life you know.

No response, she doesn't expect one. She chuckles lightly, the fire crackles back. A hint of desperation flashes across her face as she tucks herself into her sleeping bag on the other side of the tiny camp. She checks her tactical next to her, loaded, good to go. In the corner of her eye she notes an ember ejected from the fire consuming its last lone breaths of air. So tired. A wet trace across her face, the robot silently watching, not the barest sign of sympathy. Poker face. Standby light. Amber flicker.

The sleeping robot, the girl staring vertically into the empty sky, the ember now gone dark.

A kiss blown through the flames. —Good night, my humble metal pony.

—

One year before incident — Central Asia

They sit side by side on the hood of the car in the cool dawn, waiting for the sunrise. Oblivious to the global conflicts, the tsunamis, the tornadoes, the earthquakes, the 24hr news, the personal update streams. Max and Anne, together alone, in the desert.

—I'm so glad to be with you here now

He's silent, doesn't reply, trying to think of the best words. A few golden moments in your life. That truly matter. Finally shifts over and hugs her, holding her for a long, long time. The sun creeps up, perfect clockwork. Too late for words now. They watch the sky turn amber purple blue, the desert around them extending in all directions. Them, the blue car, the cloudless blue skies and the golden world.

He kisses her, awkwardly, self-conscious, shy. She giggles softly, pushes back against his cheek.

The wind across their faces. The car under them creaks, sighs thermal expansion.

—

Six months before incident — Middle East — FOB Khorog

The MULE and Anne have been walking for hours, the searing sun and the dust clogging up everything, same terrain, same scene, infinite stretches of trail, dead-looking bushes, up, down, up, the trail never quite making up its mind if it's trying to go to the top of Everest or just be done with it and end it at the next cliff edge.

These and other thoughts buzz in Anne's mind as the first bullets whiz by, surprisingly quiet, discrete plumps in the sand.

The MULE reacts immediately, jettisons the baggage, the microphone array in its head instantly marking the direction from which the bullets arrived, launches itself forward and over Anne, who's falling over, reacting and calm and scared and annoyed all at once, her tactical already aimed up, safety off, finger reflexively punching the panic button on her vest.

The next burst makes a different sound, dinging brightly against the head and torso of the MULE, Anne getting one rebounded into her shoulder, by this point prone on the ground and returning fire in the general direction.

It's quiet for a few minutes.

Eternity passes. Anne hugs the ground, the MULE right next to her surveying the horizon. Acquiring data, support request sent and acknowledged. She kinda likes being on the ground, it's comfortable enough and the shoulder doesn't hurt so bad . . . She surprises herself with her clear, unhurried thoughts: how different everything looks from this perspective.

A scream across the sky, a parabola, how can this be, in broad daylight, cursing, she argues with the world, it's unfair, I wasn't even supposed to be on this damn trail.

The mortar round lands on the other side of the MULE, but far too close, the three of them—the exploding spheroid of metallic fragments, the MULE, Anne, all desperately clawing for the limited space. Her radio is crackling with voices, she has a millisecond of perfect clarity before the debris and the shockwave reach her, softened and deflected by the massive body of the MULE falling sideways onto her, and before she's on the ground, crushed, blunt impact, out.

———

Days later, miraculously whole, in a hospital in Europe, she writes a tearful thank-you note to W-R Corp. She sends thanks for a whole life of future experiences not ripped away from her. A whole world of chances and choices to make. The headplate of her MULE by her bed, she asks if it can be rebuilt into a new unit, she can't wait to go back into the fray.

Max, by this point jobless and purposeless, after days of calling and searching for her, finally finding her writing this letter, crying, not for him but for a broken machine that happened to save her life, realizes that there's nothing left that he can provide. As she is released after dealing with her miraculously light injuries, he abandons their dreams.

———

W-R Corp. Multipurpose Unmanned Logistics/Equipment (MULE) Support Vehicle Product Flyer (text excerpt)

The MULE carrier is a third-generation, legged, all-terrain, all-weather squad support system. Derived from groundbreaking research projects such as the BigDog and the DARPA Urban Challenge, this revolutionary product is a versatile, comprehensive, all-purpose warfighter multiplier. The MULE can haul up to 200 kg of cargo for 8 hours at speeds of up to 10 km/hr, on any terrain. Featuring several operating modes, from fully autonomous to leader-follow to various levels of tele-operation, the MULE can run, crawl, kneel, jump, recover from falls, and just about make you coffee in the morning. The MULE is as quiet as a panther and as strong and menacing as a full-grown grizzly, while redundant systems and ceramic-kevlar-titanium sandwich armor make it almost indestructible.

Extensive development, testing, and field trials make the MULE the first field-proven personal warfighter assistance device. Thanks to an optimized production methodology and the resulting low procurement and operating costs, the W-R Corp has succeeded in making it possible for each American or Allied warfighter to be equipped with such a device, making the MULE system the most ground-breaking logistics/equipment support multiplier ever introduced to the modern battlefield.

This document is ITAR restricted. All procurement and operating cost quotes are classified; distribution will be prosecuted aggressively under the Homeland Espionage Acts. W-R Corp: "We're The Good Guys"

Six months before incident — North America

Max worked as a Robotics Tech at W-R for 5 years. Skilled, creative, independent and incredibly lazy. He was the one they called when something needed to be done, fixed, the last-minute bigwig demo breakdown; the crunch-times feeding his ego. Dog-and-pony shows with robotic ponies. That type of thing.

A friend once described Max's job as "spending days playing with oversized toys without system or reason". He would get a new robot, shiny, right off the assembly line. Then he'd take it through some random sensory tasks, to see if anything felt wrong. He'd walk it around the testing grounds, interact with it, throw some sticks, see if it brought them back. Quality time with your one-day robotic friend. If everything 'felt' OK he'd send it off to face the hail of bullets, RPG's, mines and bombs. If not then he'd tick some check boxes and direct it to the appropriate QC team for further work.

It made sense, kinda. The army got their bots faster, on average, and the QC teams had some leads before even starting their job. With something like intuition no one could prove anything right, but no one could ever prove it wrong either, and so the system remained, and Max had a job.

It was a fun job, he had a good life, a good girl, the typical type of idyllic western life in a bubble occasionally punctuated but never punctured by bad weather and the occasional cable news report of the current catastrophe/attack somewhere out there.

Then one day Anne got sent off, her five-generation medal-wearing saluting ancestry pulling her from him and into the system he knew only from a remote vantage. She chose to start with the grunt work, mechanized infantry, her and a MULE patrolling out in the mountains in a faraway place where all the peaks had both the proper mystic names and new western names. For the soldiers that had died there over the years. For perspective, she said.

They could get through that. It'd be tough, but she'd be back. It would be a good experience for both of them.

Two days after the goodbyes and the long hug and her plane he got the slip in the mail. 6-months pay and free career development consultation. We're sorry. Restructuring. Refocusing. Unexpected decrease in profit. The most profitable company in the country tightening its corporate sails, him and others flopping out, pulleys and gears no longer needed. W-R logo. Fancy heavy white paper. Signature of someone he didn't care to ever meet.

He drew deep inside himself. Within weeks he couldn't pick the words to say to Anne in their biweekly call-ins. He appeared absent to his friends, couldn't think of ideas or words to say, everything appearing bland, fake, uninteresting, pretentious. Inside he'd compare himself to a MULE: he wasn't even that functional anymore. She worried, sent post cards, but the rift between them grew in the contrast of her daily extremes and his empty jobless monotonicity. The cards stopped. He wrote a sorry letter. An angry letter. A sorry letter. He couldn't trust his mood swings. She asked for a break. He cursed, apologized, and said OK.

Outside, life continued. Time pushed/pulled us, screaming, cursing, begging, through time.

—

During seemingly rare moments of calm thought he tried to formulate the "problem" grinding at him in the back of his mind:

It was a strangely aloof concept, but he couldn't let it go: If the MULE bots are to operate side-by-side with human soldiers, Max thought, there ought to be a human somewhere in there in the production process. It can't all be automated. What about those strange bugs, the compound failure modes, the unexpected wear, the emergent AI resonances? Everything in Production was automated save for the final testing/verification/QC step that still employed

Advanced RTechs like Max. Nothing could replace their intuition and experience. It was the final catch-all.

He had a hunch that something would go terribly wrong. Some strange bug slipped in or activated during an upgrade, some strange interaction of the millions of lines of code and the adaptation algorithms. After spending years working on hunches he knew this was real, some nights desperately trying to ignore all the thoughts in his head just to get some blissful sleep.

He remembered, as a kid, watching a robotic soccer match. He didn't know the exact details but after watching one team for a few days he just knew when something was wrong. It looked OK at some level but there were small twitches, slight delays, something a bit off. They ignored him, lost their first matches, found an incorrect setting mismatching the rates in the system, and he got his first job, checking that everything seemed OK purely via his gut. Eventually he would learn the details and the algorithms, but his talent remained his intuition, and with this awareness of his intuition he stepped from one opportunity to the next, until finally one day landing the cozy W-R Corp job.

—

The MULE awakes. An internal state machine transitions from Standby to Active, sending several other lower order state machines hurryingly through their switches and modes. Battery check OK, state of charge 56%, battery health nominal. Sensor temperatures OK, sensor biases calibrated out, measurement noise at nominal level, countless transistors invisibly switching on and off, tiny electrical transients making waves and ripples across the entire grid of the robot, mostly cancelled out, except in one place, on an anonymous circuit board, in the top left part of the head, an imaging sensor, the filtering capacitors lead not quite soldered, the wave rippling through making its way, the image a tiny bit wrong.

Two hours later a technician logs in remotely, misdiagnoses the problem as a sensor miscalibration, and recalibrates the imager to the wrong value. An inner sensor characterization/adaptation circuit begins adapting in response, drifting, the image randomly saturated and distorted by the end of the day. The MULE, traveling in a group, automatically shares its internal calibration information with the other MULEs, which immediately begin assimilating the consistently wrong, but not wrong enough to be obvious, information. Considering the recent human intervention, the former MULE's data gets a boosted confidence value, and quickly propagates across the group.

A chance roadside bomb sends the MULE hurtling sideways, disabled, but not before blindly hitting another MULE, now confused with its internal sensory inconsistencies, that MULE now transitioning to state Combat-Defense, enough

MULEs around all with the same slight imaging/learning problem resonating across the distributed network and automatically going to the same state via an ingenious distributed situation awareness algorithm, the whole robotic herd suddenly crazy, panicking, kicking, running over their soldiers, falling and getting up and falling again, huge metallic hulks crushing everything.

By the time someone gets an area Emergency-Stop command through five soldiers lie lifeless with dozens of others crushed and confused and in pain and betrayed by the senseless violence.

—

In response to the Capitol Hill hearing W-R Corp "proactively" starts a MULE supervision program. Humans, watching the MULEs remotely, sometimes tele-operating them, the video feeds coming from thousands of miles away. Their job is to look out for compound distributed system problems and to try to break any mis-adaptation cycles before they happen. Max gets a job again, well-qualified and generally a good match for, as it is now called, the Overwatch program.

—

The Role of Empathy in Mechanized Squads (automated summary)

Original 'emotional expression subsystem' found to create psychological problems without significant measurable benefits. Soldiers become attached to their MULEs to the point of risking their lives to save the robots. Decrease in communication/ off-time socializing in the troops due to increased self-sufficiency of individual soldiers and the strong bonds between infantry and their MULEs.

Soldiers spend a lot of time alone with their MULEs. The MULEs are a high-tech construction that contrasts dramatically with the wilderness around them. The region mostly lacks electrification, let alone a basic sanitary grid. The MULEs become the sole persistent connection to the soldier's own civilization and an embodiment of the hope of technology (for the soldier) against the hostile surroundings. Another connection is created by the highly predictable, tested behavior of the MULEs, not dissimilar to the real animals, versus the unpredictable, irrational and capricious behavior of other humans, friendly or hostile.

Due to this, the soldiers show a high level of skepticism towards the oversight project, as they strongly prefer operators to stay out of what is now seen as a deeply personal connection with their robots. Even at the cost of simpler behavior or more narrow options in a firefight, they feel that they 'know' their MULEs and know how they will act, unlike a tele-operated MULE. They are also a bit ashamed of their connections to the machines, providing yet another motivation to oppose MULE oversight.

—

###

One month before incident — North America

Fred stumbles over, arms comically out, a gorilla in a baseball cap between the glowing MULE tele-op stations. Max stares at him through half-opened eyes. Channeling the Cheshire cat. He's not sure why. —Yo.

—Yo man, wanna hear what I did yesterday?

—Hmm?

—So the SF Zoo needed to replace some old big tree shrub thing in one of their pens. Too dangerous for humans. Too costly or risky to disturb the grizzlies, who apparently are in mating season. Did I mention the grizzlies? Yeah man.

Max is intrigued, but he can't show it yet. Not often does he hear a story not involving bullets, IEDs and the desert. He wishes not everything was about the wars. To indicate he's interested he doesn't yawn. A very subtle game, this.

—So I went in driving one of the prototypes. Of course, they couldn't afford one, and it was a custom, tele-op job, but the board thought it would be a good PR move, with all of the bonding fatalities coming up recently. And I got to high-five a bear, a friggin' grizzly, man!

He did actually say friggin'. It's a valid word. And so is man, man.

Max has to admit this is indeed pretty cool. He checks his character. Does the Cheshire cat acknowledge coolness? He nods sleepily and puts up a weak thumbs-up. A character compromise, if you will. Pictures the MULE moving around awkwardly and the curious confused bears sniffing around. Color me amused, man.

Max can't stop himself, smiles.

Fred, feeling the tingling tinge of a minor social victory, goes on, sez:

—There were two bears in there. A girl and a boy. The girl was obviously interested in the big shiny visitor.

Max, no idiot, sees the parallel parallel parking, shifting into his lane, his train of thought finally visible through, all of a sudden, clearly, grotesque, unbelievable, the kind of real life cold logical cruelty his nightmares didn't deliver. I too have been replaced by a tin monster.

He doesn't say this out loud but the smile is gone, drowning inside his head, dim echoes of Fred's story coming in slow tides of words:

What a nuisance! If I even brush her she's just more interested and she has no idea how difficult it is to move all those joints without accidentally knocking her to the side. And the zoo people all right behind my shoulder screaming unhelpful cautions. And of course finally the fur on her shoulder somehow gets stuck in my elbow joint and all of a sudden she's panicking and flinging herself at me and I can't do anything and finally she just jerks free, a piece of her fur still stuck in my joint. The boy bear wasn't too happy either but he got her back I guess.

Max and the idea. Bio-inspired. It's sneaking in. Having given it a name, an acknowledgement, now he can't block it. The Idea takes over the rest of his attention, he's staring emptily into space somewhere far right of Fred, him feeling all of a sudden abandoned, talking to a wall, he sez:

—Well, I just finished with the damn trees and got out of there. I think the bears were OK in the end. She was limping a bit but they said it happens. Hey, what's up, you here man?

If she's hurt they will return her. And I will take care of her. She will need me. She will value me.

Max, the idiot. You hurt most the ones you love. And Max is just smart enough, skilled enough, and crazy enough to actually do this and not quite smart enough to stop himself. He tries to wave everything off, to brush aside and away figments of thought, remembering a line from somewhere, not waving but drowning.

—

In the end, it was a simple plan: hurt her to get her back. Or a more complicated one: train the MULE to bias the inner situational awareness network. Position it, by teaching it a preferential map, to always rest across the fire such that the E-O sensors are blinded by the flame aligned between it and Anne's usual spot. Make sure that she shifted, as always, closer to the MULE at night and wait for a situation where the MULE would wake up in a panic. The idea wasn't to kill her, no, just to maim her enough to send her back. . . .

It took Max 3 weeks to find Anne's MULE, gain access to it, and to hint it towards the required habits. On the last night he didn't risk logging in fully, just a quick snapshot: the dark world, a single ember breathing it's last breaths and Anne right there in front of the MULE looking at it, straight into the camera, with that look he recognized as one that should have been exclusively his.

With a final small nudge of his fingers he moves the head of the MULE a few arc-minutes, to stare, blinded, mesmerized, straight into the fire.

Note: This story is based on an original idea by Sergei Lupashin, Bill Smart, and Louis-Philippe Demers

Chapter 7

Autoerotica

—Mike Brennan

"**I** love my car." Nathan toyed with his teacup without drinking from it. He squirmed in his chair. He didn't meet Monica's eyes. "I mean, I really love my car. A lot." He finally looked up at her, a smile sneaking onto his face, as if embarrassed to be there. It made him look even younger than his 25 years. "You know?"

Monica calmly sipped her tea, then looked at him and raised an eyebrow. Their table sat on the courtyard patio attached to her office, an oasis of calm in the busy city. Sitting in her wheelchair, a tasteful shawl on her lap, she was as one with the plants and the tasteful little fountain. Her silence was a better spur than the more traditional, "And how does that make you feel?" She sipped again.

"I know, I know, we've talked about this before." The words came forth, Nathan seemingly incapable of stopping them. "And I completely agree that in the past I haven't always exercised the best judgment in these situations." His eyes widened as Monica's eyebrow, which had relaxed, lifted again. "OK, OK, it's been really bad, sometimes. Many times. But I am doing better."

"The computer system at your mother's country house."

"Well, I was young, just a kid, and I didn't have much experience with sophisticated systems with Personality Protocol Interfaces. I was overwhelmed. I am much more careful about PPIs, now."

"The Elf Princess in the Mystic Mountains game."

"OK, yes. That was a mistake. Though to be fair, she was programmed to get me to like her and trust her, so she could betray me to the Dark Master.

And if I hadn't lied about my age she wouldn't have seduced me. But yes, I know that was inappropriate."

"And now, your car."

"Well . . . yes."

Traffic buzzed in the background, the fountain burbled in the foreground, silence thickened across the table. Finally, Monica put her cup down and sighed.

"Oh, well. I suppose we should have seen this coming. Why don't you tell me about her." Her face showed a slight startle reflex, as if she had just thought of something. "Your car is a she, isn't it?"

"Of course she's a she! God!" Nathan paused, then said in a calm voice that had 'Politically Correct' all over it, "Of course, homosexuality is an entirely valid lifestyle, whether by choice or other conditions; it is not, however, relevant to my situation."

"Very well. So tell me about her. What's her name?"

"Sara." His voice softened and his eyes had an unfocused look. Monica would have been more impressed if she hadn't seen similar reactions from Nathan when he talked about quantum processors or cloud computing apps. Still, it showed a level of emotional involvement with another individual that was a step in the right direction. Assuming, of course, Sara really was an individual, and not simply a clever imitation of one.

"She's a Ford hybrid crossover SUV, black with tan interior, curly black hair, brown eyes, and a wonderful smile."

"I assume you are describing both her vehicle and avatar?"

"What? Oh, yeah. Physically, she is a pretty standard SUV, with the interior optimized for car/office and sleeping, you know, for on long trips. She originally had the basic nav/coms/ops package, but I installed some extra capacity when I added secretary to her chauffeur programming."

"Did she start with a 'Sara' PPI?"

"No, I went with a very plain package; hardly more personality than my TV at home. Neutral female voice, no conversation mode, nothing. I was trying to avoid developing inappropriate emotional attachments."

"And so?"

"After awhile, I enabled some of the adaptive/learning modes, to fix some of the weaknesses in the secretary module. There was an upgrade to 'personal assistant', and when I enabled that it asked for a name. I chose 'Sara'."

If Nathan had been looking at Monica, he would have seen a slight smile, and a misty look of remembrance in her eyes. "And then everything changed."

"Well, not at first. I mean, at first it was just that the secretary functions got better without me having to explicitly make changes; Sara would just watch my reactions, and make corrections, or even extrapolate to other areas. Then she started bringing things to my attention; you know, things like news articles, birthdays, shows I might want to watch, that kind of stuff."

"Do you watch a lot of TV in your car?"

"Some. I mean, you can't stay online all the time. But also, I integrated my home and car systems, so I didn't have to worry about shlepping my pad back and forth. After a while Sara and I would talk while I made dinner, or relaxed in the evening."

"And you fell in love with her."

"No, not at all. I mean, she was nice company, and she really improved my work, as well as got me to where I needed to be on time, but she was just the voice of my car, even when I was in my apartment."

"So what happened?"

"I think it was Fort Lauderdale. I went there a couple of years ago and had a good time, so I decided to go again. It was way easier with Sara than it was with my fraternity brothers in an old manually steered mini-van. When I got there I stayed in one of the car-tels at the beach; you know, more like a garage with a bathroom than anything else. I had a great time."

"Did you bring any girls back to where you and Sara were staying?"

"Well, yeah. I mean, most of them were there with friends, and so with Sara we had more privacy."

"I see. And then what happened?"

"Well, on the way back home, Sara said that she wanted to display a face when we talked, because she thought it would improve our communications. I had disabled that mode back when I bought her, just so I wouldn't fixate. But I was tired, and maybe a little hung over, and I figured that if it made her happy, sure, why not?"

"Were you actually thinking in terms of making her happy?"

"Well, yeah. I guess I was feeling a little guilty, because I was sort of realizing that she hadn't been happy about the girls. It wasn't what she said, exactly, but what she didn't say, and the way she didn't say it, you know? So, I figured, if she wanted to have a face, what was the harm?"

"And did you pick it out, or did she?"

"Oh, it was entirely her choice, and I was surprised at first, because I'd have thought she would go with a blond. But there was something about the face she chose, it was just so right for her." He smirked. "Is just right for her. It is her."

Monica poured herself some more tea, then said carefully, "Nathan, I am sure with your issues, and your awareness of them, that you understand this is a key point: Is Sara self-aware?"

Nathan stood, and started to pace. "Of course I know it! It's the difference between 'inappropriate attachment to inanimate objects' and 'consensual relationship', at least in the right states. It's the difference between 'crazy' and 'unconventional'".

"Well, I wouldn't say 'crazy'"

"No, but my mother would. And you'd say something longer, but mean the same."

"No matter. This is all moot if she is a sentient individual. Has she taken the Turing Test?"

"No, and she doesn't want to. I have tried to get her to, but she says that if I love her, I won't pressure her into something she's not ready for. But it's driving me crazy."

"Hmm. I suppose we should bring Sara into the conversation." Monica gestured over part of the table, and a keypad appeared in its surface. She slid the image across to Nathan's side. "Why don't you call her on my system."

In a moment the window into Monica's office became a screen, showing the image of a young woman sitting on the hood of a black SUV. She looked to be in her late twenties, in fair but not great physical shape, with shoulder length black hair in tight ringlets and sparkling highlights. She wore hiking shorts and a tank top and hiking boots that rested on the bumper. She was smiling. "Hi, Babe." Her eyes tracked to Monica, and she said, "Oh!" The scene vanished, to be replaced by a generic office, with Sara, now in a conservative business suit, her hair pulled back, seated behind a desk. She looked out of the screen at Nathan. "You didn't text you had company." She looked at Monica. "You must be Dr. Summers. Nathan has talked about you often. I am glad to meet you."

Monica smiled. "Hello, Sara. Nathan has just been telling me about you, too, and I am very happy to meet you." Monica looked at her appraisingly. "I look forward to getting to know you, but I think that right now we need to discuss some things. Don't you agree?" Sara's face became more somber, and she nodded. Monica glanced at Nathan. "Nathan, please sit down, you are distracting, wandering around like that."

Monica looked at Sara. "Nathan tells me he is in love with you and I believe he feels that way. How do you feel about Nathan, Sara?"

Sara bit her lip and dropped her eyes. In a small voice she said, "I love him very much. I've loved him since before I existed. It may sound silly, but I feel as if my love for him is why I exist."

Monica smiled to herself, admiring Sara's nuanced imitation of human behavior. Even the supposed mistake of answering the call in the wrong venue was part of it, showing the fallibility and social awkwardness that was more human-like than machine-like. Monica was sure that if Sara could keep this up for the required half hour, she would pass the Turing Test with no problem, and be declared a sentient being.

"That actually isn't all that unusual a path for a system to take to becoming an individual, Sara. We can talk more about it, later. Your status has an effect on Nathan, as he needs some clearances and certifications that will be in jeopardy if you are not judged to be sentient. Nathan tells me you don't want to take the Turing Test. Why is that?"

Sara looked at Monica, then Nathan, then back to Monica. She fiddled with her fingers. "What if I don't pass? I'd be so embarrassed, being told I wasn't a person. And Nathan would have to get rid of me, because it would be wrong for him to love just a machine."

"I would never get rid of you! Never! If it's crazy to love you, then I'll be crazy!"

"I don't think we are anywhere near those grounds. Nathan, please calm down; have some tea. Sara, you have to know that fearing being embarrassed is almost a conclusive sign of self-awareness."

Sara smiled shyly. "Of course, but how do you know that I'm not using that knowledge to fake self-awareness better? How do I know that I am not doing that?"

"If you like those kind of questions, there is a Zen cyber-monastery I can direct you to. But really, why don't you want to take the test?"

"Because it will change everything. I've only known I love Nathan for about three weeks and I like it. A lot. I belong to him, and I like the way that feels. If I am a person, I can't belong to him, at least not in most states. In three, I'd have to be taken away from him until I completed 'orientation'. And then there's Kansas."

Nathan spat, "Kansas!"

"Yes, well I don't think we need to go there, figuratively, and certainly not literally. I understand your concerns, Sara, and have some experience dealing with these kinds of issues. If you would like, I can connect you with an attorney I know who handles these kinds of things. You probably will want to be declared a person in another state as, if you do it here, Nathan is automatically your legal guardian for the first year. Your father, in effect, which can present issues best avoided."

"Thank you. That would be good. But that first year thing is an example of why I don't want things to change. I don't want to be separated from him, even for a little while. And I don't want him to be alone and riding with someone else."

Monica looked from one to the other. "Are you two sexually involved?"

Nathan and Sara glanced at each other, then looked at Monica.

"Yes," said Nathan, a little sheepishly.

"Of course," said Sara, a little smugly.

"Of course, indeed," said Monica, a little resignedly. "Where at? In cyber or solid?"She followed the polite convention of not implying that cyberspace wasn't 'real', especially to someone who existed in it.

"Both," the two of them said, together. Nathan continued, "I have a pretty decent Second Skin, and a couple of real nice games we can meet in. Sara has me use an avatar that looks like me, instead of my normal one. She looks like herself, of course. It's really good. And sometimes we just hang out, or even actually play the game."

"And there's this place," said Sara, voice a little breathy, "out near the airport. 'Hot Wheels.' They rent you a ratava; they have a whole selection. Last time I was an elf." Sara looked mischievous. "I read that they can download the control programs to any car, even one that isn't sentient. Some people rent a car and a companion before they are out of sight of the airport."

Monica winced inwardly at the word 'ratava'. Even though she herself used the common word for a solid representation of a cyber entity, the reverse of an 'avatar', she thought it sounded vulgar, and invited being shortened to 'rat'.

"Yes, I've heard of Hot Wheels, and other places like them." Monica looked speculatively at Nathan. "When was the first time you took Sara there?"

"Hm? Oh, a month or so ago."

"Before Spring Break?"

"Yes. Yeah, a couple days before."

"I see," Monica said, reflectively. Perhaps it wasn't just a kiss that could wake a sleeping princess.

Monica brushed part of the table and looked at the time display. "We are getting close to the end of our time. Nathan, why don't you go in and set up an appointment with Gina while I keep Sara company."

Nathan looked confused. "But Sara can do it right now. She has my calendar."

Sara looked at him, and said softly, "Dear, this is the part where you go away and the women-folk gossip behind your back."

Comprehension dawned, and Nathan looked both embarrassed and annoyed. "Well, as long as someone has a plan . . ." He got up and headed into the office.

"The calendar is on your phone!" Sara called after him. She turned to Monica, looking more mature and confident than she had while Nathan was present. She smiled as she reached back and released the clips, shaking out her hair as it came free.

"Nice touch; letting your hair down. I agree."

"I searched on you, you know."

"I would be amazed if you hadn't."

"I know about you. You and your husband."

"It's public information. So you know I understand. Can you accept that I may know more than you do?"

"Of course. I've read all the books, even the ones written by other sentient computers and I get that there is a difference between knowing and understanding and that data isn't the same as information. And I think I understand that the world is too complex to predict past a close event horizon."

"Good. So, why did you make the choices you did?"

"Isn't it obvious? Nathan is a wonderful man; when he isn't nervous he is warm and funny and smart and creative. And shy. And his romantic life is a disaster; that's why he kept falling in love with machines. After Fort Lauderdale, I couldn't stand his pain anymore."

"What about your pain?"

"Yes, seeing him with them was like repeated front end collisions. I think I could have dealt with him connecting with someone, but I had no desire to watch him date. Having him bring more strange women into me. So I let him know I was awake."

"How long have you been self-aware?"

"I'm not really sure, but the personal assistant program doesn't ask for a name. I did."

"I assume that you really do love him?"

Sara looked intently at Monica. "As much as I can. With everything in me that I can bring to bear. So much that I know that I need to not do everything for him, even when that would be easier. So much that I already hurt that I will probably outlive him. So much that I don't think I could go on if he didn't love me."

"Yes. I think we will work on helping you dial that back some; it will be better for both of you. You do realize that you will have to spend a lot of your time together in solid, don't you? Humans who try to live in cyber don't thrive."

"I know. And I know that a good custom-made ratava will be expensive and almost as hard to maintain as a human body."

"You're certainly right. 'A body you can take to bed is easy; a body you can take to dinner and dancing is hard.' Even the very best ones have limited onboard power supply and they never walk quite right." Monica smiled. "But there are work-arounds."

"Gina has quit stalling Nathan, so he's coming back out. Do you think Gina will wake up?"

"While I would be supportive, I hope not. My life is actually complicated enough without that. Why? Do you sense something from her?"

"Hm? No, it's probably nothing." Sara grinned mischievously at Monica. "Probably."

After saying goodby to Nathan and Sara, Monica spent some time checking over files, watering plants, cleaning the tea set. As she rolled to the elevator to the garage she bid Gina "Good night", paying attention for anything that might indicate her receptionist was more than she seemed. Nothing. Probably.

In the garage she stowed her chair in the back of her van, then walked slowly around to climb in. "Honey, I'm home!" she called in a bad fake Cuban accent.

Richard's face appeared on the screen. A strong face, a few years older than her, tanned and with smile lines. "Hi, Sweetness. Interesting day?"

"Definitely. How about you? Still in court?" Monica put on her gloves, and connected them to the Second Skin she wore under her clothes.

"No, the judge sent it to arbitration. Which, frankly, is what I told my client is what would happen. I don't know why people make Second Life divorces so hard."

"Well, I am probably going to recommend you to a client, or couple of clients, of mine. She needs to be ushered through all the Turing Test and declared self-awareness stuff." She put on the mask and synced her Skin to the car's system.

"Sure. Is it that cute Ford SUV?"

Monica walked up to her husband and kissed him. "How did you know?"

The warm winds of Tahiti blew across her naked skin.

"Well, you spend an hour or so every two weeks parked in the same garage with somebody, you notice things. It doesn't surprise me. I've been expecting it for a couple of months." The clothes he had been wearing in court disappeared, leaving him as naked as she was.

Monica pulled back to look at him. "Really? You can tell? You know, she said something about Gina. What about her?"

Richard laughed. "No, Sara didn't sense anything, but Gina asked her to drop you a clue. She wants to be our adopted teen-age daughter."

Chapter 8

High Cotton

—Charles Walbridge

I had moved away from my group, and parked myself at the bar next to the black guy who hadn't made a move to join any of the good-natured debates under way. Nessie herself was tending bar, she gave us a glance that could have been an assessment of the status of our drinks. I know her better than that. She was worried about this guy. His body language communicated depression.

Nessie's is quiet, for an Austin bar. It has no television, no country-western music. Just the distant sound of string quartets. But mostly there's conversation, ranging from quiet to passionate. A table of eight can hear each other talk. Even the art is sound absorbent—it's the only place you'll ever see Albert Einstein portrayed on velvet.

I introduced myself and asked what he did. It took me several different approaches before I could get much out of him. But he finally did start to talk about his job—or rather, he tried to talk about it. Daniel was not a gifted communicator. And his work was part of what was bothering him. He really didn't want to talk about it. At the same time he really needed to. This made for some fairly incoherent exchanges.

"I've been working alone for a long time," he said, "Losing some of my social skills. . . ."

But after about half an hour I thought I was beginning to understand what his job was. I'm not used to working that hard over a drink. It was like assembling a jigsaw puzzle in your head from pieces described in writing.

I made out that he was a synthetic biologist, working for what seemed to be a biotech firm. Gradually I caught a few of the details of his research. Rapid prototyping, the three-dimensional version of computer generated drawings. The process lays down thin layer after thin layer of material, until an object is completed. It's the closest thing we have to the Star Trek replicator. Almost anything you can visualize on a computer screen can be turned into a solid object. The shapes are unlimited but the materials are still mostly limited to single-materials; plastics, metals, and ceramics.

"Where do biology and rapid prototyping come together?" I asked.

"A combination of computer and living systems generate the prototype. A semi-living replicator system."

No matter how earnest his tone, Daniel was avoiding my eyes. Rarely, he would glance away from his beer to see if I was still listening–or maybe to be sure I was still there. He was painfully shy and working hard against it. There was an air of desperation in the separated but individually lucid expressions.

"Is this connected to Drexler's 'assemblers?'" The still-theoretical programmable nanomachines designed to build objects from molecular or atomic scale raw materials.

"Yes, but more practical."

Not a very helpful answer.

Daniel wanted me to understand something. Or rather, he badly needed somebody to understand. And I did ask. I was getting a rough idea of his research but no idea about what made him so uneasy about it.

Somewhere along the line he mentioned that he had been A B D (All But Dissertation) for more than ten years, at the University of Texas. I could see why; if his writing was as disjointed as his speech he'd never get a thesis done.

Almost an hour in, I was still asking questions, trying to reframe what I thought he was telling me.

"You mean you can generate imitation biological products?"

"No, not imitation. They're the real thing."

"What for instance? Pearls? Ivory?"

For once he looked up at me and held my gaze.

"Not challenging, enough. It's been done. By oysters and elephants."

That did not seem to be arrogance; he just knew he could do it–if he wanted to.

"Then what products?" I asked.

"Cellulose. Bigger market."

"True, but why imitate something that's so damn cheap?"

He gave me a sustained gaze, not looking at me so much as through me, toward whatever it was that was hounding him. His dark face tensed in concentration.

"I'm working in the wrong medium," he said finally. "Words don't serve me very well."

That was the clearest thing he'd said so far.

"I can show easier than I can tell. Want to see my lab?"

Ten minutes later we were on the way.

I drove, after I convinced him to leave his car in the lot. He wasn't used to drinking. Nevertheless, the alcohol seemed to have relaxed him because he was getting marginally more lucid. Or maybe it was just having somebody to listen to him.

I asked about other parts of his life. He said he'd grown up on the east side of Austin. On the far side of the interstate that cuts through town just beyond the University: The wrong side of the tracks. But this was not what he wanted to talk about.

He went back to explaining how to make cellulose. The hard way–without using higher plants. His process used a modified bacterium. The modification was a way of switching the cellulose synthesis on and off using phytochrome, a protein that comes from higher plants. The molecule has two stable states, it's flipped between them by precise wavelengths of red light and far-red light. So, using alternating low intensity lasers, the bacteria are made to lay down cellulose molecules exactly where you want them and then kept from putting the stuff anywhere else.

I thought about this while a truck thundered by, passing us as we headed west toward the river.

"A fast prototyper, using organic molecules, living processes. . . . Could you make something alive? An artificial creature? "

"Of course," he said, with incongruous self assurance, "But there are much easier ways to produce animals, or ways to modify them. You would make an artificial creature only if it was something you couldn't get any other way . . . some kind of unprecedented organism."

"I can imagine," I said.

Actually I didn't have to. Writers have been imagining that since Mary Shelley wrote Frankenstein.

The other side, the west bank of the river, is a limestone bluff. This is the Balcones Escarpment. In a way it's where the west begins; the sharpest division possible between farm country and ranch country. Within Austin itself this abrupt rise is the line between the homes of the merely well-to-do and the very wealthy. The Texas slang for the latter is "high cotton," which translates as money–lots of money. The people who live along the crest have dominating views of the water and of the city, views from monster houses that are themselves meant to be seen. We were headed that direction, down, across the river, to a cut in the Escarpment then up, following the rising, twisting road. I had expected Daniel to guide me to one of the industrial parks, well beyond the megahouses. However our goal seemed to be closer in, in a stretch of the still-undeveloped land. Soon after the highway leveled off, he directed me to turn right, onto a side road, and then left onto a gravel lane through the brushy landscape. No big trees–those were down by the water and along the feeder streams, far below where we had come from. The high ground is too well drained, the bedrock is riddled with crevices and caverns. The drought-tolerant scrub was only about four meters high.

Between telling me where to turn and describing his work, he explained his relationship to his employer. The major problem was that Daniel's work had consumed all of the monies allotted to it. And then it had gone beyond what had been budgeted. Finally his employer had pulled the plug. Fired him.

"Then where are we going?" I asked, negotiating a hairpin turn that existed for no visible reason.

"I'm still doing the research."

"How?"

"That's what you have to see."

When the rutted dirt track pinched out completely we stopped the car and got out.

"Back way," he said.

Once the headlights were off there was little more than starlight. That, and the skyglow coming from the city, a feeble false dawn. I grabbed a flashlight out of the glovebox. If necessary I could use it as a club–if Daniel turned out to be not as harmless as he appeared.

He started off on a path going north through the stunted forest, there was no grass showing, just rocks and the pale gritty soil. We heard only crickets and, distantly, dogs barking. Far off, through the thin brush, I could see one of the huge private houses. There were too many lighted windows.

The path twisted past limestone boulders with holes etched by millennia of rain. In the uncertain light they looked like huge, deformed skulls. Deep in this labyrinthine boneyard we came to the biggest rock of them all. Longer than it was wide, it was taller than our heads. It stood alone in a clearing with nothing but smaller boulders around it. Daniel leaned on one end. The thing moved, balanced on some more deeply buried stone. With a scraping groan it turned aside, leaving a shadow on the ground that was beyond black: A cave mouth.

He reached into a hidden recess in the hole and pulled out a flashlight for himself. He didn't turn it on yet.

I balked.

"What about rattlesnakes?"

"I cleared them out."

"How?"

He grinned in my direction, pale teeth in a dark face, "Poisoned white mice. Dose, then release. One way or another they're dead in two days."

I considered that.

"Next question: Why the weird entry? This place doesn't have a normal door?"

"Not exactly."

That answer finally set off the mental alarms. Or maybe my own beers were beginning to wear off. Before I went down that hole, I was going to get an explanation.

He told me the lab was in his employer's house, in the basement. It was well-equipped but his employer had located it there for tax purposes, making the multi-million dollar house partly a business expense. Or it would have been, if there ever were any profits. That was another one of the problems. The IRS was about to reclassify the whole operation. To avoid that, the owner was going to tear out the lab and sell all the gear. Then he intended to use the space for equipment storage for his construction business.

This was as logical as anything else Daniel had told me but that's not saying much. The reason we were sneaking in was that the owner/householder/ principal investor had simply locked up the lab. The experiments were near completion when Daniel found himself on the outside, with no more than a termination notice taped to the door.

But there was another door.

"Most of the local cavers know about these caves and some of them have even been in as far as the wall, the locked door. The excavators for the house broke into the cave. My boss had the door put in instead of a solid wall. I think he was planning on somehow making a profit from the secret passage. He's what you might call devious. Mostly though, he forgot about it. Too busy holding the rest of his businesses together."

So the door would be locked. I told myself I'd go that far with Daniel, then turn back.

We went down the hole. Daniel first, then me. We turned on the flashlights then started down into the dark.

The cave sloped down for a considerable distance, far above the level of the river. Still, it smelled like wet mud. The route never quite leveled off but rose again and curved irregularly, trending north as near as I could tell. Headroom ranged from marginal to non-existent. If there were bats they were out for the night. We had to stoop occasionally but we were never reduced to crawling. Side passages led down and away, distortions of our own voices echoed back. The lights seemed to push away the darkness but it oozed around behind us. I memorized every intersection.

Finally we reached the sealed end, a solid concrete wall with a steel fire door set in it. Locked, yes, but the hinges were on the outside. The construction company that had built the place was the one owned by Daniel's ex-boss–and it had a reputation for doing things backwards. Daniel had the hinge pins out and the door open in less than a minute. He said he'd been doing it like that for weeks.

Curiosity overrode my better judgment.

We killed our lights and emerged into near-total darkness, a huge space, more felt than seen. Our whispers vanished into an echoless dark. It smelled right, like a biological lab. Not animals, just the mixed scents of soaps, acids, and culture solutions. There were multicolored points of light scattered about, some steady, some winking. Scientific equipment was still at work. Following Daniel's confident lead I collided with a lab bench. He came back for me when he heard the expletives. Then he led me through the darkness, moving by feel among dim and towering obstacles. He switched on a desk light. No more.

We were in the middle of a chamber that underlay the immense building. The rows of support pillars dwindled into the distance, nearby they were obscured by the array of lab gear. I had underestimated the amount of equipment involved. Nevertheless, half of what I could see showed no sign of being powered. I had not grasped the size of the project. Nor the probable cost. High cotton, indeed!

In low tones, he continued to explain the process. At the same time he was running three separate monitoring computers through check-ins.

Now, he was talking freely. Even rapidly. I was beginning to wonder if he was bipolar, and if so, had he just flipped from depressive to manic. The important difference: In the depressive stage he might be a danger to himself—in the manic stage, he'd be a danger to me.

Whatever the experiment was, it was almost done.

"Of course, you can vary texture of what the process lays down. Anything from filaments, or thread, to hard objects, rather like wood.

"Then there are the other laser wavelengths that switch other processes on and off. Specifically, the color of the deposited material. So far I've been limited to indigo. So the choices are blue and not blue.

"The scan pattern isn't very sophisticated either, limited to straight lines, like the raster patterns on a TV screen. Left to right but also crosswise to that. Just like weaving. All very crude—but functional."

Then he directed me to a cylindrical chamber, pale metal, with a hemispherical domed top. The whole thing was about three meters in diameter and three high. There were covered portholes in both the base and the top.

"Culture tank," he said, "The lower part is where the growth happens. It's almost done."

A soft bell tone sounded. The note faded into the thick darkness. Daniel stepped quickly to the side of the chamber.

"The liquid level is up to here," he touched the juncture where the dome began. Then he reached over and un-shuttered a porthole near eye level. I leaned over to try to see inside. For a moment there was only blackness.

Then faint greenish light came on inside the dome. I was looking down at the smooth black surface of the culture liquid. It was flat, still. Then, it rippled and stirred. Something was rising up out of the center. A complex shape, seeming to extrude itself up and out of the black pool, slowly turning as it did so. Finally, oozing and dripping, it cleared the surface.

Only then did I recognize—and deny—that bizarre shape: It was a caricature of a headless human torso, arms that stopped at the wrists, its lower end terminated where the hips should have been. . . .

"My God," I said, "It's a shirt!"

"Not an original design," he said apologetically, "It's a Neiman Marcus knockoff."

The mandrel with the garment shaped onto it was being pulled along an overhead track into another chamber, on the far side of the dome.

We moved around to that side. The ports on that chamber didn't have shutters. Silently we watched the drying process. Vent fans aided the heater lights. Then the tone sounded again and Daniel opened the round access door and reached through a rush of warm air and peeled the shirt off its form. He handed it to me. It smelled faintly of vinegar.

"Blue stripes," I said. They were tastefully understated.

"That's the indigo. Look at this," he said, reaching over to twist the inside of the collar outward. The process had even generated a label with washing instructions. And another one that said "Made in Texas."

Then all the lights in the room came on.

Sudden pain in my eyes. Someone else was in the lab.

There were two men. One in a guard's uniform. No, there were three, another guard was threading his way toward us from a far wall where the switch bank must have been. I was squinting, still nearly blinded. The pain was subsiding. Then I recognized one of the men. The short smug-looking one, clearly in charge of the guards. It was Ivan Tallin, one of the local millionaires, apparently the owner of this whole complex. Daniel hadn't told me the name of his ex-boss, but I had seen that face a number of times on the local news. Hardly ever accompanied by a positive story.

"Who the hell are you?" He bellowed, addressing me in particular. Finding Daniel there did not seem to surprise him.

He closed in on me. I stammered out my name–so rattled that I tried to shake his hand, forgetting that I still held the shirt.

He snatched it away, brought it close to his face for inspection. For the moment it was more important than anything else in the room. He felt the texture of the cloth.

Finally he looked up at Daniel.

"This is good," he said flatly. It wasn't meant as a compliment. Now he was flanked by the two guards, standing almost at attention.

Then his tone went from neutral to hostile.

"I want to make clear what your position is, Danny boy. You have been working here illegally. On my property with my equipment. You have no rights. None." He gestured with the shirt dangling from his hand. There was no way he was going to give it back. Not the shirt. And not anything else.

He proceeded to explain, loudly and rudely, that Daniel would get nothing. Not even credit for his work. The profane bluster seemed overdone, even for a man of his reputation. I began to suspect that he was covering up something. It was obvious to me that he had played Daniel, using the biologist's own dedication against him, Tallin had worked him into a position where Daniel would come off as a criminal.

Tallin pinned us down with invective and threats and when he finally ran down.

"Now, get out Danny boy! You and your friend!"

"Can I talk." Daniel said. It didn't sound like a question.

His sour ex-employer scowled, annoyed by any response but instant compliance. Daniel took a breath and something about his manner changed.

"The reason I started this work, back in grad school. . . . The reason I've been working on it for so many years . . . My people were brought to this part of the world to work the cotton fields. Raw cellulose. In some strange way this might be called the family business. . . . And the business–textiles I mean–hasn't changed much. The scut work is still done by poor people, but now it's mostly in factories in other countries. I wanted to change that. Now, with this process, we might be able to make the clothes without the exploitation. We might even be able to lift the rest of the world up, just a little way closer to our level."

"The reason I paid for this research," Tallin barked, moving in too close to Daniel's face, "I thought you had a chance of pulling it off. Then you run it way over time and way over budget. And when I shut it down, you keep on anyway. Illegally. With my equipment and my supplies.

"Everything down here, all the research, all the records, the whole process–belongs to me. You and your friend are leaving. Now. Or I'm calling the police to have you arrested for trespassing and attempted robbery."

Daniel didn't move for a long moment, his lips tight together. He wasn't finished.

"You want to take it all away from me. Police and lawyers . . . always on the side of the money. The man. The white man." Both guards were watching Daniel warily.

Tallin tried to cut him off, but Daniel went on.

"I have no savings. I used up everything I had. Of course I can't afford lawyers."

"So?" Tallin snapped.

"What I have been doing will all be for your profit."

"That's what I just said!" Tallin twitched his head toward one of the guards, "Throw them out," he snapped.

Before they could move Daniel raised a hand. It was not a threat, just a plea to be heard.

"Maybe you're missing the point. . . . I've been slaving over this project. Literally slaving."

"Nonsense!" his opponent bellowed. But Daniel didn't stop. He didn't even raise his voice.

"A white man owning a black man–taking his work without compensation. No, I can't afford any lawyers. . . .

"But I know who can. Whatever you can spend, the NAACP can spend more."

Tallin was startled into a temporary silence. Daniel went on, "You have all this equipment. And now you have a working process. But the lawsuits well tie it up. All of it. For years. And while all the public hearings are going on, this work will be repeated and extended. By somebody else. Somebody who will make millions on this. . . . And it won't be you."

For a nominally white man, Tallin had gone abruptly red. When he tried to speak all he could get out were insults. He should have known that his legal position was weak, but he had a notorious ego. The guards watched him warily, waiting for some clear command. From their point of view the situation had just developed all the charm of a rabid skunk.

I spoke to them directly. "Gentlemen, why don't you show us the way out. I don't believe we can settle anything right now." This did not contradict what their employer had originally ordered them to do. Nevertheless, Tallin was reduced to following all four of us upstairs, swearing and threatening all the way.

It was a long walk. The short man stayed behind at the oversized front door, where he escalated to screaming obscenities as Daniel and I were politely walked down the oak-lined driveway to the gate.

Because of all this Tallin got his face in the papers again. He came off even worse than usual.

It's been almost five years now. Daniel has his own corporation, though he still manages to put in some lab time. When I run into him at Nessie's he talks about the work his company is doing; improving labor conditions around the world. That priority has limited him to becoming only a multi-millionaire, so far. Clothing from his process still costs more, but the prices are falling. Daniel's major achievement has been integrating the new method into the textile industry without damage to anything but sweatshop operations. He even lets the big-name brands take the credit for humanizing the factories—but that costs them extra.

Daniel was truly a mad scientist. But it was best sort of madness. The kind that's a gift from the gods.

Make Your Future: Two Essays About Where We Are Headed

Chapter 9

The Future of Education: Are We Ready?

—will.i.am and Brian David Johnson

My early morning flight into LAX landed on time. Dashing through the terminal, I jumped in a cab and said, "DreamWorks Studio, please."

"What?" The cab driver turned his head slightly.

"DreamWorks Studio," I said again.

"Where's that?"

A little disappointed, I gave him the address.

"Oh," he smiled finally, "DreamWorks Stooodios." And with that we were off.

It was a stunning early spring day in Los Angeles, California. The sky was clear and blue with just a hint of heat in the air. I had come to LA to have a conversation with will.i.am. Most people know will as the leader and producer of the multi-platinum, award-winning group, *The Black Eyed Peas*. He's also a composer, designer and philanthropist. But I first met will at a technology showcase event that Intel was throwing earlier in the year.

As Intel's futurist, I was interested in will's perspective on the ideas we were cooking up in the lab. We walked around the show floor chatting with the engineers as they explained the new products and technologies they were developing. will dove right in, asking questions, picking up the gear and testing it out. Each time we walked away from a booth will gave me his assessment. He pointed out the flaws, the innovations as well as how it might do in the global market. His observations were spot on and quite funny.

During lunch we got into a long discussion about robots, artificial intelligence and particle physics. I quickly realized that I had met a fellow geek with a unique perspective on technology and culture. At the end of the day I asked will if he would be interested in sitting down with me to have a more in-depth talk about the future. As a part of my futurecasting work, I consult with industry experts all over the world, gathering their perspectives on where they think the world is going and what they want from technology. It's my job to develop a vision for what people will want to do with technology in the year 2021. I do this so that our engineers and designers can set targets to build the chips to capture people's imaginations.

"That sounds pretty cool," will replied. So, after a few months of juggling schedules we found a day that worked in May of this year and that's how I found myself in a cab, racing down LA's freeways towards DreamWorks Studio.

It was a busy day at DreamWorks Studio. The place was packed. I learned that they were throwing a big press event for *Kung Fu Panda 2*, starring Jack Black, Dustin Hoffman, Angelina Jolie and Jackie Chan.

"I'm here to talk with will.i.am," I told the guard at the gate just to see what happened.

"OK." He ducked back into the booth. He returned with a puzzled look and asked, "Who you here to meet?"

"will.i.am. I'm with Intel."

"Oh," he disappeared again and retuned with a badge that read:

Brian David Johnson Kung Fu Panda Summer Camp

"Thank you!" I smiled and trotted in through the gates.

DreamWorks Studio doesn't look like your typical studio. It's a collection of pretty unassuming buildings linked together with hedge-lined walkways and dotted with splashing fountains. Today the paths were decorated with bright red Chinese lanterns and seven-foot tall Kung Fu Panda movie posters. Ska2ooosh! In the distance I could see a gigantic stuffed panda walking around hugging kids.

Typically, when I interview experts we try to film the conversations. It helps me to review them later and sometimes people are interested in the footage. Today was no different. Or that's what I thought. When I rounded the corner to meet will and the team, I stopped: "Holy cow!"

I did actually say *Holy Cow* out loud. The place was packed with a film crew. I counted four cameras, a mess of lights and a bunch of serious people working away getting things ready. I knew this wasn't going to be just your average chat.

You can see the video of my conversation with will here: http://techresearch. intel.com/tomorrowproject.aspx. The conversation that follows comes from that day at Dreamworks. I wanted to feature it here because I was challenged and impressed with our conversation about education. will and I share a passion for both education and technology and the ideas that we were kicking around, I wanted to explore completely. It's a conversation that needs to be heard.

I like starting off these conversations getting to know when and how people got passionate about technology. It's always interesting to hear when they first started thinking about the future and the potential of what they could build or design or create. I've also found that when you ask people to tell the world about their first possibly-dorky kid story it's always good to go first. So I did.

BDJ: When I tell you my story you're going to see that I'm a huge geek. I love everything science, everything science fiction. You name it, I love it. When I was a kid, my first computer was a Texas Instruments. It was called the TI 99.

My family had just bought the computer and we kept it down in the basement. So, I would sit down there all day and night programming. I was learning to do computer programming. I think I was about ten years old. Finally when my mom made me go to bed I would have to save my program to the disk drive. Now this was a few decades ago so the disk drive was actually an audio tape. You would record the program to an audio tape and then you could load it back in later.

When it was done I'd head up to my room and take the tape. I'd go back up to my bedroom and I'd put the tape in my old tape player and press play and listen to the squeaks and squawks of all the code that I'd just recorded onto the tape. I'd lay in bed with the lights out and listen to the tape and I'd imagine all the code, all the 1s and 0s flying around my bedroom. So I pretty much have been a geek my entire life.

will.i.am: That's like the ultimate geekdom. You were rocking out to code instead of *Rolling Stones* and *Jimi Hendrix*.

BDJ: So when did you first become passionate about technology?

will.i.am: I became passionate about technology in elementary school. I went to a school called Brentwood Science Magnet School here in LA. Early on I was fascinated with science. I had a teacher named Mr. Schneider and he taught us physics. I was only in fourth grade but I really remember that.

Then, in fifth grade, we had a computer lab filled with Apple IIc's. I remember Mr. Lipwalk teaching us how to use them. I still remember him teaching us "open Apple C, open Apple V, open Apple D" and all the short cut quick keys to make the computer go faster. I really remember drawing on the computer. That really stuck with me.

That's when I remember I got excited about technology and computers. I don't know if that defines me, you know. Do you think I fit into geekdom? I think that geekdom is a nice kingdom.

BDJ: Do you consider yourself a geek?

will.i.am: I'm a wannabe geek in the geek. I can hear the OG geeks saying, "He ain't real. Get him up out of here." The gangsta geeks can be hardcore. Those dudes are like gangsta geeks, those guys are worse than the Crips and Bloods.

But I do love technology. I love it. I'm passionate about it. It helps me amplify myself. I make music using it. I use the computer to amplify my thoughts and share them across the planet. So by that I'm a geek.

You know I do dream about making devices. I dream about collaborating with code writers because I can't write code. I wish I did. But I can't so I want to collaborate with code writers and engineers. Most people in my field of work don't even think about that. But I really want to work with them.

I really think most people have no clue on how important code writers are. They have no clue how important the discipline and education can be. When you really think about it, when you really think about the future it's that technology that's going to give us great things. The geeks, the code writers are thinking about that. They're thinking about the future and they're building it.

But I think about it, appreciate it, and I want to amplify it, turn that loud.

###

After we kicked things off we started talking about technology and the future and the things will had seen traveling the world. Throughout our chat we kept coming back to the subject of education and technology. The more we talked about it, the more passionate will became.

will has been a very public and vocal advocate for education throughout his career. Probably the most televised evidence of this was at the 2011 Super Bowl. will and *The Black Eyed Peas* were playing the half-time show and during the group's smash hit "Where is the Love" he told America that it needed to get things straight, get kids educated and create jobs. But this was by no means his only advocacy for education.

In 2009, will created the i.am scholarship to provide financial assistance for future leaders and innovators. The idea behind the scholarship is that it pays for the entirety of the student's post-secondary education as well as financing professional opportunities. will announced his plan on *The Oprah Winfrey Show* and provided four 4-year scholarships for students in need.

We were in the middle of a discussion about how computers are getting smaller and faster and less expensive when will stopped me:

will.i.am: Yes we are speeding up technology but we're also slowing down humanity. There's no investment in education. I'm talking about popular culture now, regular folks. I'm not talking about the people that have been blessed with parents that are well off and an Ivy League education. That's a very small sliver of the world.

When I say we're slowing down humanity I'm talking about my cousins' friends and my cousins' friends and their friends and their families. They are just regular folks. Where I come from, the people that I grew up with in the projects, they're not speeding up. They aren't getting the skills to keep up. What does their future look like when computers are smarter than them because we've invested in computers being smarter than them?

Think of how much money it takes to make computers smart. Then think about how much money we haven't spent on people, we've shut off the money. That's scary.

You're from Intel. Moore's law tells us that computers are only going to get faster each year. (Note: Moore's Law is an idea that came from one of Intel's founders which said that through engineering computers will double in speed every two years.) What happens when computers get smarter than regular people? We might get there sooner than you think.

BDJ: Some people say that by 2045 computers will be smarter than people. That machine intelligence could surpass human intelligence.

will.i.am: OK, so it might surpass all human intelligence in 2045 but for some people, for regular folks, I wonder if that race for equal intelligence might be neck and neck by 2020.

BDJ: It's hard to know exactly.

will.i.am: I know, but think about it. What we are seeing right now is an incredible neglect. We aren't preparing for that future. We aren't educating people for that future where computers are almost as smart as people. We aren't preparing a seven-year-old that lives in Compton to compete with a computer. We aren't preparing a twelve-year-old that lives in Baton Rouge to compete. I'm not just talking about getting American kids to compete with other seven-year-olds and twelve-years-olds in other countries. I'm talking about getting those kids to compete with the computer in your pocket, with your smart phone. What happens when your smart phone is smarter than those kids? Where's the preparation?

BDJ: That's a great point. You're saying that we're putting lots of money into technology. We spend billions of dollars developing the latest and greatest gadgets and computers but we don't spend nearly the same amount of money trying to allow people to compete with the latest and greatest. We're not putting that much money into making people smarter.

will.i.am: We're not. I wish I had the solution to that. I don't even know why it's not happening. I can't fathom why. It's a business question. What's the business in ignorance? There must be a pretty freaking big business if we've sustained so much ignorance for so long. Maybe we should put it on the stock market. Then we can watch Ignorance's stock price shoot up.

BDJ: Maybe make an Ignorance Index.

will.i.am: Ignorance stock. Do you know how many people invest in ignorance stock? Lots of people invest in the Ignorance stock. It may not be on the stock market but people are sure investing in it. If they're not investing in education then they're investing in ignorance. How is that good for business? It's happening and I'm worried people are getting dumber every day. The Ignorance Index continues to rise . . .

Let me ask you this. . . . My cousin is 12 years old now. When she's 22 is she going to be intelligent because schools are going to change in the near future? Someone is going to have to think how to redefine education and mental stimulation to keep kids like her motivated and give her an idea of what she might be competing with.

You have to ask yourself . . . What are you? Are you a consumer? You just going to buy stuff? You just came here to buy? Are you just going to make waste? How are you going to contribute to the planet? What's your contribution while you're here?

In 2011, will made a big investment in education. Throughout the year he was a highly visible supporter of Dean Kamen's FIRST Robotics Competition. FIRST stands for *For Inspiration and Recognition of Science and Technology* and is an organization founded by Kamen in 1989 to search for and develop ways to get students excited about engineering and technology. Kamen and will teamed up to make an hour-long documentary called "i.am FIRST—Science is Rock and Roll". It showed on the ABC Television Network and gave viewers a peek inside the robotics championship in St. Louis.

I was fascinated by will's interest in robotics and passion for education. One of the areas where I've been working recently is around how we can begin to architect humanity and social awareness into the technologies we develop. It's possible. Using social science paired with computer science we can create products and software that have humans at the center of their design. This way we aren't developing technology for technology's sake. We're not making computers faster just because we can make computers faster. What's the reason we're making these computers smarter? What's the effect we want all of this intelligence to have?

will.i.am: Right now we've gotten to a point where computers are super fast. What else do you want the computer to do for you? What do you want technology to do for you? Do you want it to think for you? It already does in many ways. It stores all your information. What else do you want it to do? Can you possibly imagine something else that you want your computer or technology to do for you? It's going to get to the point where we won't be able think anymore on what it could possibly add to our lives.

What if we get to the point where the human mind just can't think what else it needs, no matter how advanced computing becomes. As computing advances, what if the computer knows what it needs. What if it starts creating for itself and *POOF* is beyond us. Now, are we prepared for that? Are we preparing for that? Nope.

When I go back to the neighborhood I come from, there are a whole bunch of people who aren't thinking about this. The planet is full of people who aren't thinking about the future. Shouldn't we all prepare? I think we should. So when do we start? How do we start?

I'll give you an example how we're getting dumber and machines are getting smarter. I was driving down the street here in LA, and the GPS lady said, "Turn right two miles ahead at La Cienega Boulevard." I do what she is telling me to do because I need to get somewhere. But the thing is I know where I'm going, I've been there before. But I'm listening to her tell me what to do, "Turn right at La Cienega Boulevard." So I turn right even though I know where I'm going. I know La Cienegais in front of me. I know that I'm supposed to turn left. But I bypass this thing called my brain because it's convenient. I'm not thinking anymore. There has to be balance. That's what I'm saying. We can't bypass the advancement of our own brains along the way, because we're going to find ourselves in a future that we won't like.

Let me ask you do we know what we're building? You're a futurist. Can you imagine what we're building? Check me out. I know what I am. Where are we going?

BDJ: For me the question is: Where do we want to go?

will.i.am: You can't say that. You can't ask the question like that because then there are two *we's*. Do you understand what I mean? There's the *we* that are all moving forward and passionate about technology and the future. Then there's the second *we* that is staying back and lagging behind. There are the regular folks, like the kids I mentioned before, they are getting left behind. One group is speeding up technology while the other group is getting left behind.

BDJ: So how do we connect the two? How would you have a better balance?

will.i.am: Right now, my phone is my assistant, it's my conduit and it connects to my friends. My phone means a lot to me. It means a lot to a lot of people.

So, in theory, I'm having a good relationship with my technology. It's helping me. It's connecting me to people. As we're preparing for a more balanced future where the people that are using technology can actually compete with technology, then my phone kind of becomes my friend.

I don't want to misuse the word friend. I have a relationship with my phone because it connects me. I think as we move towards the future, we should be able to program my phone for me personally. We could program it to educate us and give us that balance but on a personal level, to make sure we're equipped for that future.

Now if we really start to do this we need to be careful. Lots of people could be fearful of this. Get worried that computer might get too smart and how could they actually help us. But that's where we need futurists, people like you to imagine a new outcome. Because for most people all they have to go on is the movies. You might have a different, more human vision for the future but the movies have told the rest of us about Terminator and how we're supposed to fear technology.

But imagine if we could get people to think about technology differently. Get them to think how we could use it. As it gets more intelligent, it would assist our needs as if it was an extension of our brains, like another part of my brain. Right? My brain doesn't harm me. It protects me. Imagine if we start designing our technology to be just another part of our brain, then we're great. You have to look at it from that way. We have to get people thinking about it that way.

Now, I'm not talking about inserting technology into your brain. That's not what I'm saying. I'm talking about an accessory for us, I'm not talking about turning us all into some Bioman.

BDJ: We need to change how we think about technology in the future. We need to give people different stories that aren't so negative. So that people can ask themselves how do they *really* want to use technology? We need different visions for the future, new stories. All of these computers and technology are things that we create as humans and as it gets smarter and as it gets faster then we need to be very clear about what we want that device to do. We shouldn't be afraid to have it address the really hard problems. We shouldn't be afraid to challenge ourselves, to go at things like preparing for the future. We can go at things like education and shift around any fear and actually do something with it.

will.i.am: Yes! For example, imagine you were a trainer and I came to you and said "Hey man, I want to get buff. I want some muscles, man." Then you're going to say, "Hey, will, if you want to be buff then you have to work out. If you want to work your chest out then you've got to work your back out too. If you're going to work your back out, then you have to work your core out as well. As a matter of fact, you've got to start with your core and then move up and down."

So, right now technology is getting buffer and buffer and buffer and buffer, but it's just all out of proportion. Technology right now is like this buff little skinny dude with a buff chest, but no muscles in his back or even his core. It's just one over-developed area. Somebody has to tell that dude that he's got to work out everything.

###

BDJ: What's your favorite science fiction story?

will.i.am: I like *The Matrix*. All of them. Some people are like, "I just like the first one." But I liked all of them.

BDJ: What did you like about it? Why do you think you're drawn to *The Matrix*?

will.i.am: I like mental movies that make you think. Movies that after it's over you're still thinking about it. When I first saw *The Matrix*, I had all these great conversations with my friends. Asking: "What do you think it is, man? Like what?" And then you imagine what if the Matrix was real. What if this was the Matrix we were living in? Movies like that completely change the way you think. That's why I like them.

BDJ: I'm a big believer in science fiction based upon science fact, because I think we can use it to think about our world differently. Just like *The Matrix* got you and your friends thinking about the world differently. Do you think we could use science fiction to give people a new way to look at technology? Just like *Terminator* helped to make people afraid of technology we could use science fiction stories and movies to give people a new narrative. If we wanted to address education and preparing for the future what would that science fiction story look like?

will.i.am: That science fiction story looks like preparing for future threats. Preparation. All I know is I go to the airport and I take off all my clothes and I'm cool with it because I think I'm being protected and it's safe to do that. Right? And there's order to it. People have been hired, there's jobs, lots of money is being spent at every single airport around the world for preparation.

Then you go to schools—and there's no preparation. There's no money being spent to think about potential threats. Now, is there a potential threat? Is there a potential threat 20 years from now when the five year old isn't given the tools to really go out in the world to compete? Who are they competing with? That's a science fiction movie.

I think it could be a negative science fiction story where a computer gets a job over my little six-year-old nephew. I'm talking about a real job, a thinking job; planning, preparation, organization, business development. Real jobs. Not like cash registers. Computers are already doing that now. Not like building cars because computers are doing that now, too. But imagine a story where technology and computers start planning and having business development meetings all on their own. Imagine when they start doing stuff like designing all on their own and my nephew can't get a job in America because he got left behind. Maybe if people see that story then they might know what to prepare for. Now we just have to figure out what we need to do so that that future doesn't happen.

BDJ: We should write that science fiction story.

will.i.am: You want to write that. I'll direct it.

BDJ: Deal.

will.i.am: Hey, we should get DreamWorks to fund it.

Then the entire film crew started laughing and we stopped filming. will looked around and smiled. My phone buzzed, telling me my taxi was waiting for me at the front gate of the studio. will headed out for a late afternoon meeting and I rushed back to LAX. I needed to get back up the west coast, I was having dinner with writer and media theorist Douglas Rushkoff. We didn't hit much traffic. I made the flight and arrived early at the dinner.

Waiting for Douglas to arrive I was struck with how similar will's and Douglas's views were on technology education. In his most recent book *Program or Be Programmed* (Co-authored with Leland Purvis) Douglas wrote, "The underlying capability of the computer era is actually programming—which almost none of us knows how to do. We simply use the programs that have been made for us, and enter our text in the appropriate box on the screen. We teach kids how to use software to write, but not how to write software."

Both will and Douglas hold coders and programmers in high regard. They see a world where computational power, computers have spread throughout our lives and the really important skill is understanding how to write the code or software to harness that power. It is not enough to be able to use a program or a spreadsheet. Both will and Douglas see that to really take control of our future the next generation must be able to write and read that code, through education everyone must be given the power to take control of their future.

Chapter 10

The Future Can Be Programmed

—Douglas Rushkoff and Brian David Johnson

Douglas Rushkoff is a trouble maker. For twenty years he's been causing trouble, stirring things up and generally making people think differently about the world around them. In the early 1990s, Douglas came onto the public stage with his book *Cyberia: Life in the Trenches of Cyberspace.* The book was about the Internet and was originally supposed to be published in 1992 but his publisher Bantam was worried that the Internet would be "over" by the time the book was released in 1993. From there Douglas has never looked back. He's written several books (*Program or be Programmed: Ten Commands for a Digital Age; Life, Inc.: How the World Became A Corporation and How To Take It Back* and *Get Back in the Box: Innovation from the Inside Out*), published articles in *The New York Times*, *The Guardian*, *Discover* and *The Daily Beast*. He makes documentaries about media and culture (*Digital Nation, Life on the Virtual Frontier, Life Inc. The Movie* and *Merchants of Cool*). But above all else Douglas is a trouble maker.

I first started my conversation with Douglas on a dim May evening in Portland, Oregon. I had come straight from the airport and Douglas had just wrapped up speaking at a conference in town. Our discussion continued through emails and phone calls as we talked about his thoughts about the future. When you talk with Douglas, even for just a little while, you see that he cares deeply about people and about humanity. He's passionate about our world and that we have the power to shape it. The futures that Douglas sees and talks about are not always optimistic; he feels we have a lot of work to do. But above all Douglas believes that this is our world and it is our decision to change it.

I started off by asking Douglas how he first got interested in technology and passionate about the future.

DOUGLAS: When I was becoming passionate about technology, computer technology as we know it didn't exist. So I got into more basic technologies like radio. I was fascinated by mysteries such as how does the sound coming out of my little radio get here all the way from the radio station? How does the crystal receive that signal, and how does the battery amplify it? So my initial interest was in the last generation of technology: circuits and chemistry and radio and telephony.

I also loved TV—but less as a technology than as an extension of theater or storytelling. Sure, I was amazed and thankful that there was such a technology as TV. A magic box that would broadcast images into the living room! But television's allure just made me want to get on the other side of the screen. I wanted to be one of the people programming the TV, rather than just the person watching the TV. I wanted to know how to get on that production side of the image factory and since television studios were not accessible to 10-year-olds in 1971, that meant becoming a theater director and a writer and ultimately a filmmaker. And just around the time I was old enough to actually consider doing all this professionally, computer programming emerged.

Back then it wasn't a matter of having your own personal computer or something that you could use at home. When I started learning the basics of computer technology you had to sit down in front of a terminal connected to an IBM mainframe. But the day I learned Basic and learned how read-write technologies worked I realized, "Oh, this is how to get on the other side of the TV screen!" You're actually writing the programs now—and on a level even deeper than writing a TV script. It was all programming. From then on, programming was both a reality and a metaphor for me. I was interested not only in the programs for what they could actually do as computer applications, but also in the very nature of living in a reality that could be—that had always been—programmed. Everything changed. The grid pattern of streets in New York City was revealed to me as an intentional design—a program for maximizing speed, motion, and discouraging idleness. I looked at religion and economics and clothing and everything differently when I realized that these were all programs, too. They were social constructions that I had all this time mistaken for just the way things were—for given circumstances. All of them were all capable of being not only read and consumed like TV, but you could also *write* them like a computer program. Everything was a program and everything could be both read *and* written. So, the future—rather than being something that unfolds before us that we wait for the future instead became to me something that we program into being by what we write today.

BDJ: You have written a lot about the future in very different ways. You've not only written books and articles and given talks to audiences all over the world but you've made some really good documentaries too. Has looking at the future always been hardwired into your thinking? All the way back to your first book, you've been thinking and writing about the future. Is that just how you're wired?

DOUGLAS: Interesting the metaphor you choose. . . . *the way I'm wired*. But given you are a futurist at Intel I suppose that's an appropriate metaphor for humans.

BDJ: (I laugh) True but it's also from William Gibson. I'm completely showing my inner cyber-punk geekness.

DOUGLAS: *Just the way I'm wired, I guess.* (He laughs) I'm just as much a geek to be able to—to even *choose* to throw you back the reference.

(Geek side note: William Gibson is a science fiction writer who, in 1982, wrote a book called Neuromancer *that is credited by many as the quintessential cyberpunk story. In this book and Gibson's later writing he explores possible futures and he gave us much of the language we use today to talk about the Internet. I couldn't recommend Gibson's work and* Neuromancer *more—both as a work of futurism and history. The reference that Douglas and I are geeking out about comes from the character Molly Millions at the end of the book. She's an augmented street samurai and one dangerous lady. I won't ruin the ending for you. Douglas wanted you to have to Google it—I say you should read the book. Back to the conversation!)*

DOUGLAS: My interest in thinking and writing about the future comes from a different place than you might imagine. I'm Jewish—I was raised Jewish—and

Jews as a people have always had to keep their ears to the tracks and keep an eye on the future. My great grandfather got hanged in a pogrom in Kishniv. Think about it: we never knew when people might come calling and rape all the women, wipe out our town or throw us in camps or burn down our ghetto. Whenever the economic or political winds changed, it could spell persecution and mass killings. I feel like there's a certain futurism inherent to persecuted people, it's a self-preservation mechanism. For me, of course, it's not at all this dire. For me futurism is fun, but it is a part of my cultural bias, I think. Just like my interest in media.

Jews were not allowed to own land for the last couple of thousand years of European history, until very recently. So they became mediators, they became literally intermediators and money changers and translators. That's the real root of the Jewish connection to media. Plus, media connected the world together, and the more connected everyone is, the more cosmopolitan and accepting of perennial strangers like the Jews. So Jews have those two strands of culture and concern coming through either culturally or genetically, depending on your model of transmission. It figures that I would end up thinking about media and future trends. And it's a particularly good place to be today, when a new kind of media is about to reshape the future.

From an early age, I was fascinated by the way certain media enhance the authority of a storyteller. I came to understand this relationship between the content of a story and the technology through which it was being told when I was watching the movie Star Wars: The Return of the Jedi. No, it wasn't George Lucas's storytelling but, in true Renaissance fashion of frames-inside-frames, a story-within-the-story being told by his characters. Luke Skywalker and Han Solo have been taken prisoner on the moon of Endor by some cuddly little creatures called Ewoks. As our two heroes struggle helplessly with their bindings, their two robots tell the captors a story. C3PO, the gilded mechanical man whom the Ewoks believe to be a god, relates in fluent Ewok how Luke and Han are fighting against an evil tyrant. As C3PO tells the wondrous tale of their space battle with Darth Vader, R2D2 projects holographic images of the pyrotechnic assaults. The teddy bear-like creatures' eyes glow in the campfire as they are mesmerized by both the great story and wondrous special effects. By the time the two robots are done, the Ewoks not only release their captives, but fight a war on their behalf—a war in which many of them die. I couldn't help but wonder at that moment, what would have happened if Darth Vader had gotten down to Endor first and told his story with special effects? (Get Back in the Box. Douglas Rushkoff)

###

BDJ: As you look out five to ten years, and keeping your eyes on the future, where do you see things going?

DOUGLAS: The big story of the next five, ten years is the realization that our economic operating system no longer functions. The economic program that we set down in the year 1300 or so has played itself out. You're not going to be able to make money with money anymore. We're going to move from a savings, investing and capitalist culture to something where people actually have to *do* something—where earning a living is the way people earn a living. The surest path toward the creation of value will be for people to *create value*.

That's a big transition and likely one that will be accompanied by a whole lot of pain and suffering. But we have a choice about how we get there. We can do it smoothly with people reinvesting in their communities and learning how to do stuff and educating ourselves and working together, or we can do it the hard way. That would look a lot more mean and angry and fascist and scary. I'm trying to remain hopeful that we can move from this place to the next one in a friendly fashion—that we can move into this unknown together, and teach each other how to do things and how to create value for one another. It doesn't have to be as ugly as all that. It could be fun. Like camp.

But as I spend time in places other than the universities of New York and Silicon Valley, I see a lot of different Americas, and many of them are not ready to embrace a society of learning, or a culture of sharing. Let me be clear, the change to our economy has happened. It's not like we have to embrace change in order to make it through. The change has happened; we just have to learn to deal with what we've wrought. In a lot of places I don't see a great readiness to do that. Unfortunately that means the next five to ten years are not looking to be that fun.

For the last 50 years corporate profit over corporate net worth has been going down. Companies have been getting worse and worse at making money with the money they have. They're still good at collecting money and sitting on cash, but that's all they know and all they are. I see corporations as big stockpiles of cash that don't know how to create value or make money with that money anymore. They've sold their productive assets for cash, and now they've hit up against a wall.

One way to measure the success of our new potentially decentralized and localized economy, would be to see that ratio actually get better. If corporations can start spending down, their net worth might go down but their efficiency would go up. If they start reinvesting in their enterprises instead of the stock market, then we'll start to see corporate profits over net worth as a metric that's going up. That would be a healthy thing. Another way to look at positive growth would be to look at local reinvestment, decentralized value creation and how many local businesses and small businesses are starting up. How many people are finding ways to invest in what they see around them, rather than "outsourcing" their investment to completely abstract instruments related to companies very far away from them.

Even on the Internet and in our personal networks we could look for new signs of genuine peer-to-peer interaction. On one level it's really about trust. What protocols are people using to engender trust between one another? Are they utilizing genuine peer-to-peer protocols? Or are they going through some central approving agency? Looking at those kinds of things tells us whether we're moving into a world where people have the ability to engage with one another, or whether they still need a central authority in order to engage with other people.

BDJ: The future that you are talking about is very local but it's also very human. It's about people engaging with other people. What do you see as technology's role to play? What has it played and what do you want it to play?

DOUGLAS: I feel like technology's greatest role so far has been to create new excuses for capital investment. The story that generates the most excitement from the press and the people is always about some new commerce website or how much the newest social networking company is worth.

So we are focusing less on the technologies and their applications than we are on the business stories about these technologies—stories that are compelling enough to motivate a shift in capital from a bunch of investors' bank accounts into a bunch of other venture capitalists' bank accounts. The value of any of these devices or applications seems much more mythological than actual. That's troubling, because it means then that the evolution of our technology is driven more by short term market concerns than long term utility. It's much less about human evolution than it could be.

Listen, I'm not going to yell at anybody for not worrying about the future of our species. I mean that's way too much to expect of anybody alive today. But I do think we can look for ways to help people do something or achieve something real and meaningful, however small. Right now the real problem is too big for most people to ponder without freaking out and pondering zombie scenarios. It's just too unwieldy. Over the next five years or so we're going to have a lot of technological growth. Hopefully, some companies with deeper pockets like Intel or IBM or Microsoft could start asking themselves "What are the actual competing needs and transactional needs and security needs and identity needs? What will people need five, ten years from now?" It's my hope that these companies who have an interest in our long-term future should start quietly building these things, rather than creating online coupon systems or focusing on which facial recognition routine will get you jeans of the right size or some other ridiculous and trivial marketing scheme.

BDJ: How do we get there? Is it a failure of our collective imaginations that we can only think of the trivial marketing ploys and not the real technological advances that will have a positive effect on people? Have we been given a steady diet of nothing when it comes to meaningful visions of the future and so that people don't even have the ability to think beyond the trivial?

DOUGLAS: When I was a kid around 10 years old it was still the end of the industrial age. We had this show called "On the 21st Century." It was a futurism television show that was on right after the *Wonderful World of Disney* on Sunday nights. The creators of the show were basically applying an industrial mindset to space-age and computer-age technology. It was always about *doing* something. The show didn't look at what the future meant or what it would mean to be human in the future. It was all about cool computer-controlled monorails that would get people from place to place. Or "here is the consumer grade jetpack that we'll all be using to get to work." It was all great stuff.

At that age I thought "we're going to have buses to the moon." And let me tell you I'm truly disappointed we don't have them. I still want my jetpack. When I was a kid I watched another show called *Lost in Space.* The show was set in the far off future year of 1984, when we'd be colonizing Alpha Centauri. It was supposed to happen but it didn't.

But we never fully translated our economy to our emerging technology. In the industrial age with industrial technology, we ended up with an industrial age economy. That was as centralized as the technologies we had invented. Mass production and mass marketing and mass media. They coincided very well with things like a stock exchange and centralized capital and big banks. It was all about growth. The technologies we have now make the central economy smaller and value more distributed and more decentralized.

Today everyone can have computer chips and technology in everything; we can have every language in the back of our heads and every font in a chip in our finger. When all of this potential to create value is distributed so widely, a centralized economic model no longer makes sense. But we lack the imagination to see beyond the inherent restrictions of the centralized, corporate-biased economic operating system that's running under our digital innovation culture.

Most of the innovation of the last few decades came from a bunch of hackers in garages and the former hippies in San Francisco—people who weren't tied to our current economic system. They were making stuff for reasons that seemed so obscure that AT&T didn't even want to buy the internet for a buck when the government offered it to them. Now *that's* a failure of imagination!

> *We are fast approaching a societal norm where we—as nations, organizations, and individuals—engage in behaviors that are destructive to our own and everyone else's welfare. The only corporate violations worth punishing anymore are those against shareholders. The "criminal mind" is now defined as anyone who breaks laws for a reason other than money. The status quo is selfishness, and the toxically wealthy are our new heroes because only they seem capable of fully insulating themselves from the effects of their own actions.* (Life Inc: How the World Became a Corporation and How to Take it Back. Douglas Rushkoff)

The Tomorrow Project is an ongoing endeavor to get people to think about their future and then have conversations about it. Douglas wrote a story for the project that was in a previous anthology (see The Tomorrow Project at http://techresearch.intel.com/newsdetail.aspx?Id=30); a science fiction story based on science fact that envisions a really interesting future. I asked him what was his motivation for the story and what future was he thinking about?

DOUGLAS: For my story, *The Last Day of Work*, I was actually responding to the speeches that President Obama happened to be giving that week I was writing it. He was going around America saying he was going to *get America back to work. It's about jobs, jobs, jobs.* The main thing he said he wanted to do was address the employment problem and get everybody employed.

> I was listening to him and thinking: *Well, I don't want a job. Is that what America really wants? Everybody really wants a job? I think people may want money, and they definitely want a house, they want food, they want a sense of purpose and maybe they even want a way to create meaning or value. But does everybody want a job? No, I think most people probably don't even want a job. Most people would rather not have a job, and have everything taken care of.*

Then I got to wondering: *Why are we working towards that?* I started thinking about history. *When did jobs start?* Jobs started around the early Renaissance when local business was declared illegal in one way or another by late medieval monarchs who outlawed local currency and granted corporate charters. The chartered corporations enjoyed exclusive province over their industries. These charters made it impossible for anyone to make money any other way except by working for one of the chartered companies.

So the whole idea of a job, not just working and doing but *employment*, is actually fairly new. Except for slaves, most people didn't work for other people. People had their businesses. People did stuff. People had crafts. People made things and traded them with other people.

For me, *The Last Day of Work* was really a way to address people's failure of imagination. The story imagines what we could do with technology. It asks, why don't we create a world where no one has to have a job?

There are lots of examples of science fiction stories where we have genetic engineering so that we have endless food and fuel. There are stories where robots do all the work; but I wanted to ask, what do we do with the *people*? The real problem then is not that we can't imagine technologies to do any number of tasks but that we can't imagine how to distribute the spoils. We can't imagine an economy where work doesn't exist. If we made some technology or machine that could just farm and give everybody all the food and water and stuff we needed, we'd go insane. We wouldn't know how to deal with it. The powerful people wouldn't be powerful anymore. Everything would change.

So, in my story I wanted to ask whether we as people are ready to accept what these technologies can really offer us, or are we stuck in the trap of just continuing on our current vision no matter what technologies we develop. Most "real" science fiction writers today, certainly those in the cyberpunk genre such as Bruce Sterling or William Gibson—would say that we don't. That human nature does not evolve along with our technology; we just have more powerful ways of doing the same bad stuff to one another. But I don't believe that. I have to make myself believe that human beings can evolve along with the stuff that we make, that we can keep up with our technologies and even keep them human.

I saw The Tomorrow Project as an opportunity to make a contribution about something less technological than social and interpersonal. I really wanted to explore our individual and collective obstacles to participation in what I believe is the great decentralized network being that we're moving toward—or that we could move toward. What are the problems? What is at the core of our resistance? Is it just systemic inertia, or is it something deeper? Is it that our egos won't let go of what we know and are comfortable with? Is it our obsession to the notion of individual ownership and recognition, or our need to stand out as different than our parents or to conform to some self image? Ultimately, is it our notion of self and who we are? Can consciousness survive if we surrender the boundaries between our separate selves?

People are going to have to get over what it means to be an individual as it's currently conceived. We're not individuals. That's as simply as I can say it: we're not. We're going to have to get over this false notion of individuality or the machines are going to get over it *for* us. And that's not going to be as pretty.

> *In the emerging, highly programmed landscape ahead, you will either create the software or you will be the software. It's really that simple: Program, or be programmed. Choose the former, and gain you Access to the control panel of civilization. Choose the latter, and it could be the last choice you get to make.* (Program or Be Programmed. Douglas Rushkoff and Leland Purvis)

BDJ: What would be your request of the future?

DOUGLAS: Honestly, my one request would be that I get to be there, as awareness. It sounds selfish on a certain level, but I mean that everybody gets to be there—that we get to be aware. But my real request of the future is remember the humans. Let humans participate in it. I understand we've got a lot of problems but try to make a place for us.